G000123626

Carol Petley is the co-founder of the Waggy Tails Club. Waggy Tails is a place where teenagers with special needs work with dogs to increase their confidence and develop their social skills.

Visit www.waggytailsclub.co.uk.

Q&A

BIBLE VERSE
5-YEAR JOURNAL

spck

CAROL
PETLEY

First published in Great Britain in 2017
Second edition published 2019

Society for Promoting Christian Knowledge
36 Causton Street
London SW1P 4ST
www.spck.org.uk

Copyright © Carol Petley 2017, 2019

All rights reserved. No part of this book may be reproduced or transmitted in
any form or by any means, electronic or mechanical, including photocopying,
recording, or by any information storage and retrieval system, without
permission in writing from the publisher.

SPCK does not necessarily endorse the individual views contained in its
publications.

Scripture quotations are taken from the New Revised Standard Version of the
Bible, Anglicized Edition, copyright © 1989, 1995 by the Division of Christian
Education of the National Council of the Churches of Christ in the USA.
Used by permission. All rights reserved.

British Library Cataloguing-in-Publication Data
A catalogue record for this book is available from the British Library

ISBN 978–0–281–08323–7

1 3 5 7 9 10 8 6 4 2

Typeset by Fakenham Prepress Solutions,
Fakenham, Norfolk NR21 8NN

Printed in India by Replika Press

To my mum and dad

1

January

In the beginning when God created
the heavens and the earth . . .
Genesis 1.1

What is one thing you might begin this year?

20 ___ •_____
_____
_____

20 ___ •_____
_____
_____

20 ___ •_____
_____
_____

20 ___ •_____
_____

20 ___ •_____
_____
_____
_____

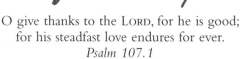 

O give thanks to the LORD, for he is good;
for his steadfast love endures for ever.
Psalm 107.1

How has God's love been a comfort
to you today?

20 _____ •_____

_____

_____

20 _____ •_____

_____

_____

20 _____ •_____

_____

_____

20 _____ •_____

_____

_____

20 _____ •_____

_____

_____

_____

3

January

To equip the saints for the work of ministry,
for building up the body of Christ, until all of
us come to the unity of the faith . . .
Ephesians 4.12–13

What would others say was your
greatest strength?

20 _____ .

_____

_____

_____

20 _____ .

_____

_____

_____

20 _____ .

_____

_____

_____

20 _____ .

_____

_____

_____

20 _____ .

_____

_____

_____

January

For surely I know the plans I have for you, says
the LORD, plans for your welfare and not for
harm, to give you a future with hope.
Jeremiah 29.11

Do you feel God may be nudging
you in some way?

20 _____ •_____

_____

_____

20 _____ •_____

_____

_____

20 _____ •_____

_____

_____

20 _____ •_____

_____

_____

20 _____ •_____

_____

_____

5

January

'Truly I tell you, unless you change and
become like children, you will never
enter the kingdom of heaven.'
Matthew 18.3

What might you do – that is spontaneous
and fun! – this week?

20 _____ •_____

20 _____ •_____

20 _____ •_____

20 _____ •_____

20 _____ •_____

January

Devote yourselves to prayer, keeping alert
in it with thanksgiving.
Colossians 4.2

How easy do you find it to 'devote yourself to
prayer' and how do you feel afterwards?

20 ___ •

20 ___ •

20 ___ •

20 ___ •

20 ___ •

7

January

The LORD will keep your going out and your
coming in from this time on and for evermore.
Psalm 121.8

In what ways do you detect
God's loving care for you?

20 _____ •

20 _____ •

20 _____ •

20 _____ •

20 _____ •

January

But Samson . . . rose up, took hold of the doors of
the city gate . . . pulled them up . . . carried them
to the top of the hill that is in front of Hebron.
Judges 16.3

What major task have you
accomplished recently?

20 _____ •_____

_____

_____

20 _____ •_____

_____

_____

20 _____ •_____

_____

_____

20 _____ •_____

_____

_____

20 _____ •_____

_____

_____

9

January

Jesus said to them, 'Come and have breakfast.' . . .
Jesus came and took the bread and gave it to
them, and did the same with the fish.
John 21.12–13

What would you like to ask Jesus
over breakfast?

20 _____ •_____

20 _____ •_____

20 _____ •_____

20 _____ •_____

20 _____ •_____

January

10

You must understand this . . . let everyone
be quick to listen, slow to speak, slow to
anger; for your anger does not produce
God's righteousness. *James 1.19–20*

When was the last time you reacted with
anger? Did it help matters or not?

20 _____ •_____

_____

_____

20 _____ •_____

_____

_____

20 _____ •_____

_____

_____

20 _____ •_____

_____

_____

20 _____ •_____

_____

_____

_____

11

January

He . . . heard a voice saying to him, 'Saul, Saul, why do you persecute me?' He asked, 'Who are you, Lord?' The reply came, 'I am Jesus, whom you are persecuting.' *Acts 9.4–5*

Have you (or do you know someone who has) had a spiritual encounter with Christ?

20 _____ •_____

20 _____ •_____

20 _____ •_____

20 _____ •_____

20 _____ •_____

January

12

I will greatly rejoice in the LORD, my whole
being shall exult in my God; for he has
clothed me with the garments of salvation.
Isaiah 61.10

Did you have reason to 'greatly rejoice' today?
If so, why?

20 _____ • _____

_____

_____

20 _____ • _____

_____

_____

20 _____ • _____

_____

_____

20 _____ • _____

_____

_____

20 _____ • _____

_____

_____

13

January

And this is the boldness we have in him,
that if we ask anything according to
his will, he hears us. *1 John 5.14*

What is your most urgent prayer request
right now?

20 _____ •_____
_____
_____

20 _____ •_____
_____
_____

20 _____ •_____
_____
_____

20 _____ •_____
_____
_____

20 _____ •_____
_____
_____
_____

January

14

The LORD is my strength and my shield; in him
my heart trusts; so I am helped, and my heart
exults, and with my song I give thanks
to him. *Psalm 28.7*

Which song or piece of music always
uplifts you?

20 _____ •_____

_____

_____

20 _____ •_____

_____

_____

20 _____ •_____

_____

_____

20 _____ •_____

_____

_____

20 _____ •_____

_____

_____

15

January

'Or what woman having ten silver coins, if she loses one of them, does not light a lamp, sweep the house, and search carefully until she finds it?' *Luke 15.8*

How tidy is your house and how much does it matter to you?

20 ___ •_____

20 ___ •_____

20 ___ •_____

20 ___ •_____

20 ___ •_____

January

16

Draw near to God, and he will draw near to you. Cleanse your hands, you sinners, and purify your hearts, you double-minded.
James 4.8

How are you trying to draw near to Jesus?

20 _____ •_____

_____

_____

20 _____ •_____

_____

_____

20 _____ •_____

_____

_____

20 _____ •_____

_____

_____

20 _____ •_____

_____

_____

17

January

Trust in the LORD with all your heart,
and do not rely on your own insight.
Proverbs 3.5

Are you struggling to trust God for
anything at the moment?

20 _____ •_____

_____

_____

20 _____ •_____

_____

_____

20 _____ •_____

_____

_____

20 _____ •_____

_____

_____

20 _____ •_____

_____

_____

January

18

Now Sarah said, 'God has brought laughter for me; everyone who hears will laugh with me.' *Genesis 21.6*

Who was the last person to make you laugh?

20 _____ •_____

_____

_____

20 _____ •_____

_____

_____

20 _____ •_____

_____

_____

20 _____ •_____

_____

_____

20 _____ •_____

_____

_____

19

January

And not only that, but we also boast in
our sufferings, knowing that suffering
produces endurance. *Romans 5.3*

Looking back, what painful experiences do
you feel may have deepened your faith?

20 _____ •

20 _____ •

20 _____ •

20 _____ •

20 _____ •

January

'Go therefore and make disciples of all nations, baptizing them in the name of the Father and of the Son and of the Holy Spirit.' *Matthew 28.19*

Who do you know who might be open to hearing more about your faith?

20 ___ •_____

_____

_____

20 ___ •_____

_____

_____

20 ___ •_____

_____

_____

20 ___ •_____

_____

_____

20 ___ •_____

_____

_____

21

January

Make a joyful noise to the LORD, all the earth;
break forth into joyous song and sing praises.
Psalm 98.4

Where do you most enjoy worshipping God –
in church, at home, amid nature . . . ?

20 _____ •

20 _____ •

20 _____ •

20 _____ •

20 _____ •

January

22

Love is patient; love is kind; love is not envious or boastful or arrogant or rude. It does not insist on its own way; it is not irritable or resentful. *1 Corinthians 13.4–5*

Who in your life are you struggling to love as you would like?

20 ____ • _____

_____

_____

20 ____ • _____

_____

_____

20 ____ • _____

_____

_____

20 ____ • _____

_____

_____

20 ____ • _____

_____

_____

_____

23

January

You shall not make for yourself an idol,
whether in the form of anything that is in
heaven above, or that is on the earth beneath.
Exodus 20.4

What are the things that make you feel secure,
and why?

20 ____ •_____

_____

_____

20 ____ •_____

_____

_____

20 ____ •_____

_____

_____

20 ____ •_____

_____

_____

20 ____ •_____

_____

_____

January

24

Now during those days he went out to the mountain to pray; and he spent the night in prayer to God. *Luke 6.12*

When do you like to pray?

20 ____ • _____

20 ____ • _____

20 ____ • _____

20 ____ • _____

20 ____ • _____

25

January

And the Lord's servant must not be
quarrelsome but kindly to everyone, an
apt teacher, patient. *2 Timothy 2.24*

Who do you find it challenging to be kind to
and why might that be?

20 _____ •_____

_____

_____

20 _____ •_____

_____

_____

20 _____ •_____

_____

_____

20 _____ •_____

_____

_____

20 _____ •_____

_____

_____

January 26

Now when Job's three friends heard of all
these troubles that had come upon him . . .
They met together to go and console
and comfort him. *Job 2.11*

What is troubling one of your friends
at the moment?

20 _____ •_____

_____

_____

20 _____ •_____

_____

_____

20 _____ •_____

_____

_____

20 _____ •_____

_____

_____

20 _____ •_____

_____

_____

_____

27

January

The LORD takes pleasure in those who fear him,
in those who hope in his steadfast love.
Psalm 147.11

Who do you love unconditionally?

20 _____ •

20 _____ •

20 _____ •

20 _____ •

20 _____ •

January

28

Do not seek your own advantage,
but that of others. *1 Corinthians 10.24*

Who did you put before yourself today?

20 _____ •_____

_____

_____

20 _____ •_____

_____

_____

20 _____ •_____

_____

_____

20 _____ •_____

_____

_____

20 _____ •_____

_____

_____

_____

29

January

And he dreamed that there was a ladder set up
on the earth . . . and the angels of God were
ascending and descending on it.
Genesis 28.12

What was happening in the last dream
you can remember?

20 _____

20 _____

20 _____

20 _____

20 _____

January

30

'He set off and went to his father . . . his father saw him and was filled with compassion; he ran and put his arms around him and kissed him.'
Luke 15.20

When God draws near, how do you feel –
excited, overwhelmed, at peace . . . ?

20 ____ •_____

_____

_____

_____

20 ____ •_____

_____

_____

_____

20 ____ •_____

_____

_____

_____

20 ____ •_____

_____

_____

_____

20 ____ •_____

_____

_____

_____

Submit yourselves therefore to God.
Resist the devil, and he will flee from you.
James 4.7

Did you feel tempted today
(and did you give in)?

20 _____ •

20 _____ •

20 _____ •

20 _____ •

20 _____ •

February

1

My spirit abides among you; do not fear.
Haggai 2.5

What tends to make you fearful?

20 _____ •_____

_____

_____

20 _____ •_____

_____

_____

20 _____ •_____

_____

_____

20 _____ •_____

_____

_____

20 _____ •_____

_____

_____

_____

February

I lift up my eyes to the hills – from where will my help come? My help comes from the LORD, who made heaven and earth.
Psalm 121.1–2

God knows we need human friends too. Who are the people who support you spiritually?

20 ___ •_____

_____

_____

20 ___ •_____

_____

_____

20 ___ •_____

_____

_____

20 ___ •_____

_____

_____

20 ___ •_____

_____

_____

February

3

For everything that becomes visible is light.
Therefore it says, 'Sleeper, awake! Rise from
the dead, and Christ will shine on you.'
Ephesians 5.14

How do you get yourself motivated
in the morning?

20 _____ •_____

_____

_____

20 _____ •_____

_____

_____

20 _____ •_____

_____

_____

20 _____ •_____

_____

_____

20 _____ •_____

_____

_____

4

February

My child, if your heart is wise, my heart
too will be glad. My soul will rejoice
when your lips speak what is right.
Proverbs 23.15–16

Who are the people who are proud of you?

20 _____ •

20 _____ •

20 _____ •

20 _____ •

20 _____ •

February

5

'Be on your guard! If another disciple sins,
you must rebuke the offender, and if there is
repentance, you must forgive.'
Luke 17.3

Do you need to forgive someone? Why?

20 _____ •_____

_____

_____

20 _____ •_____

_____

_____

20 _____ •_____

_____

_____

20 _____ •_____

_____

_____

20 _____ •_____

_____

_____

6

February

Keep your lives free from the love of money,
and be content with what you have; for he has
said, 'I will never leave you or forsake you.'
Hebrews 13.5

How happy do you feel with your
standard of living?

20 _____ •

20 _____ •

20 _____ •

20 _____ •

20 _____ •

February

7

[God] saved us and called us with a holy calling,
not according to our works but according
to his own purpose and grace.
2 Timothy 1.9

What do you believe is God's calling for you?

20 ____ •_____

_____

_____

_____

20 ____ •_____

_____

_____

_____

20 ____ •_____

_____

_____

_____

20 ____ •_____

_____

_____

_____

20 ____ •_____

_____

_____

_____

February

By the rivers of Babylon – there we sat down
and there we wept when we remembered Zion.
Psalm 137.1

Is there a matter in your life at the moment
that is causing you anguish?

20 ___ •_____

_____

_____

20 ___ •_____

_____

_____

20 ___ •_____

_____

_____

20 ___ •_____

_____

_____

20 ___ •_____

_____

_____

February

February

9

'For all of them have contributed out of their abundance; but she out of her poverty has put in everything she had, all she had to live on.'
Mark 12.44

Of the things you spend money on, what would you find hardest to give up?

20 _____ •_____

_____

_____

20 _____ •_____

_____

_____

20 _____ •_____

_____

_____

20 _____ •_____

_____

_____

20 _____ •_____

_____

_____

10

February

Then the LORD said, 'Go in this might of yours
and deliver Israel from the hand of Midian . . .'
He responded, 'But sir, how can I deliver Israel?'
Judges 6.14–15

Do you feel you are more a leader
or a follower? Why?

20 _____ •_____

_____

_____

20 _____ •_____

_____

_____

20 _____ •_____

_____

_____

20 _____ •_____

_____

_____

20 _____ •_____

_____

_____

_____

February

11

So that you also may know how I am and what I am doing, Tychicus will tell you everything. He is a dear brother and a faithful minister in the Lord.
Ephesians 6.21

Who is the (living) Christian you most admire?

20 ____ •

20 ____ •

20 ____ •

20 ____ •

20 ____ •

12

February

Making a whip of cords, he drove all of them out of the temple ... He also poured out the coins of the money-changers and overturned their tables.
John 2.15

Who was the last person to make you angry?
Why did they make you angry?

20 _____ •_____

20 _____ •_____

20 _____ •_____

20 _____ •_____

20 _____ •_____

February

13

Two things I ask of you; do not
deny them to me before I die.
Proverbs 30.7

If you could ask God for any two things,
what would they be?

20 _____ •_____
_____
_____

20 _____ •_____
_____
_____

20 _____ •_____
_____
_____

20 _____ •_____
_____
_____

20 _____ •_____
_____
_____

 **14**

February

I sought the LORD, and he answered me, and
delivered me from all my fears. Look to him, and
be radiant; so your faces shall never be ashamed.
Psalm 34.4–5

Looking back, can you think of ways in
which God has protected you?

20 ____ •_____

_____

_____

20 ____ •_____

_____

_____

20 ____ •_____

_____

_____

20 ____ •_____

_____

_____

20 ____ •_____

_____

_____

February

15

Now you have observed my teaching,
my conduct, my aim in life, my faith,
my patience, my love, my steadfastness.
2 Timothy 3.10

What aspects of the way you live do you think
speak to others of your Christian faith?

20 _____ •_____

_____

_____

20 _____ •_____

_____

_____

20 _____ •_____

_____

_____

20 _____ •_____

_____

_____

20 _____ •_____

_____

_____

16

February

Now Israel loved Joseph more than any other
of his children, because he was the son of
his old age; and he had made him a long
robe with sleeves. *Genesis 37.3*

What, if anything, causes you to feel
jealous of someone else?

20 ____ •_____

_____

_____

20 ____ •_____

_____

_____

20 ____ •_____

_____

_____

20 ____ •_____

_____

_____

20 ____ •_____

_____

_____

February

17

In his anguish he prayed more earnestly,
and his sweat became like great drops of
blood falling down on the ground.
Luke 22.44

When was the last time you prayed
earnestly for something?

20 _____

20 _____

20 _____

20 _____

20 _____

18

February

Beloved, I do not consider that I have made
it my own; but this one thing I do: forgetting
what lies behind and straining forward
to what lies ahead. *Philippians 3.13*

What things have you managed
to leave behind you?

20 _____ •

20 _____ •

20 _____ •

20 _____ •

20 _____ •

February

19

Do not boast about tomorrow, for you
do not know what a day may bring.
Proverbs 27.1

How good are you at living in the moment?

20 _____ •_____

_____

_____

20 _____ •_____

_____

_____

20 _____ •_____

_____

_____

20 _____ •_____

_____

_____

20 _____ •_____

_____

_____

20

February

Make me to know your ways, O LORD; teach me your paths. Lead me in your truth, and teach me, for you are the God of my salvation.
Psalm 25.4–5

When you think about the direction your life is taking, how do you respond?

20 _____ •

20 _____ •

20 _____ •

20 _____ •

20 _____ •

February

21

For in him all things in heaven and on
earth were created . . . all things have been
created through him and for him.
Colossians 1.16

What gadget do you most appreciate? Why?

20 _____ •_____

_____

_____

20 _____ •_____

_____

_____

20 _____ •_____

_____

_____

20 _____ •_____

_____

_____

20 _____ •_____

_____

_____

_____

22

February

'The days will come when the bridegroom
will be taken away from them, and
then they will fast in those days.'
Luke 5.35

Have you tried fasting? If so, what was
your experience?

20 _____ •_____

_____

_____

20 _____ •_____

_____

_____

20 _____ •_____

_____

_____

20 _____ •_____

_____

_____

20 _____ •_____

_____

_____

_____

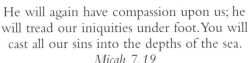 February

He will again have compassion upon us; he
will tread our iniquities under foot. You will
cast all our sins into the depths of the sea.
Micah 7.19

Is there something, for which you've been
forgiven, that you struggle to let go?

20 _____ •_____

_____

_____

20 _____ •_____

_____

_____

20 _____ •_____

_____

_____

20 _____ •_____

_____

_____

20 _____ •_____

_____

_____

24

February

Be persistent whether the time is favourable
or unfavourable; convince, rebuke, and
encourage, with the utmost patience
in teaching. *2 Timothy 4.2*

Who inspires you spiritually?

20 _____ •_____

_____

_____

20 _____ •_____

_____

_____

20 _____ •_____

_____

_____

20 _____ •_____

_____

_____

20 _____ •_____

_____

_____

February

25

Meanwhile the church throughout Judea, Galilee, and Samaria had peace and was built up . . . it increased in numbers.
Acts 9.31

How is your church trying to attract new members?

20 _____ •

20 _____ •

20 _____ •

20 _____ •

20 _____ •

26 February

I cry aloud to God, aloud to God, that he may
hear me. In the day of my trouble I seek the
Lord . . . my soul refuses to be comforted.
Psalm 77.1–2

When was the last time you felt desolate,
and why?

20 _____ •_____

_____

_____

20 _____ •_____

_____

_____

20 _____ •_____

_____

_____

20 _____ •_____

_____

_____

20 _____ •_____

_____

_____

February

27

For by grace you have been saved
through faith, and this is not your own
doing; it is the gift of God.
Ephesians 2.8

Where did you see grace exhibited today – at
home, at work, in the media . . . ?

20 _____ ● _____

_____

_____

20 _____ ● _____

_____

_____

20 _____ ● _____

_____

_____

20 _____ ● _____

_____

_____

20 _____ ● _____

_____

_____

 **28**

February

The LORD, your God, is in your midst . . .
he will rejoice over you with gladness, he will
renew you in his love; he will exult over
you with loud singing. *Zephaniah 3.17*

When do you find it easiest to spend time
in God's company?

20 _____ •

20 _____ •

20 _____ •

20 _____ •

20 _____ •

February

29

Contribute to the needs of the saints;
extend hospitality to strangers.
Romans 12.13

When was the last time you were shown
hospitality?

20 _____ •_____

_____

_____

20 _____ •_____

_____

_____

20 _____ •_____

_____

_____

20 _____ •_____

_____

_____

20 _____ •_____

_____

_____

_____

1

March

Let the word of Christ dwell in you richly; teach
and admonish one another in all wisdom; and with
gratitude in your hearts sing . . . songs to God.
Colossians 3.16

Which part of the church service
nourishes you most?

20 _____

20 _____

20 _____

20 _____

20 _____

March

When you pass through the waters,
I will be with you; and through the rivers,
they shall not overwhelm you.
Isaiah 43.2

Who are the people who find your
presence reassuring?

20 _____ •_____

_____

_____

20 _____ •_____

_____

_____

20 _____ •_____

_____

_____

20 _____ •_____

_____

_____

20 _____ •_____

_____

_____

3

March

Praise the LORD!
O give thanks to the LORD, for he is good;
for his steadfast love endures for ever.
Psalm 106.1

Can you think of a new way of praising God?

20 _____ •_____

_____

_____

20 _____ •_____

_____

_____

20 _____ •_____

_____

_____

20 _____ •_____

_____

_____

20 _____ •_____

_____

_____

March

Cast all your anxiety on him,
because he cares for you.
1 Peter 5.7

What are the issues you're wrestling
with at the moment?

20 _____ •_____

_____

_____

20 _____ •_____

_____

_____

20 _____ •_____

_____

_____

20 _____ •_____

_____

_____

20 _____ •_____

_____

_____

_____

March

For everything there is a season . . .
a time to weep, and a time to laugh;
a time to mourn, and a time to dance.
Ecclesiastes 3.1, 4

What mood(s) have you been in today?

20 _____ • _____
_____
_____

20 _____ • _____
_____
_____

20 _____ • _____
_____
_____

20 _____ • _____
_____
_____

20 _____ • _____
_____
_____

March

As they were going along the road, someone said
to him, 'I will follow you wherever you go.'
Luke 9.57

What sacrifices have you made to follow Jesus?

20 ____ •_____

_____

_____

20 ____ •_____

_____

_____

20 ____ •_____

_____

_____

20 ____ •_____

_____

_____

20 ____ •_____

_____

_____

March

Recalling your tears, I long to see you
so that I may be filled with joy.
2 Timothy 1.4

Who do you long to see?

20 _____ • _____

_____

_____

20 _____ • _____

_____

_____

20 _____ • _____

_____

_____

20 _____ • _____

_____

_____

20 _____ • _____

_____

_____

March

He who planted the ear, does he not hear?
He who formed the eye, does he not see?
Psalm 94.9

When did you last feel that God
wasn't listening to you?

20 _____ •_____

_____

_____

20 _____ •_____

_____

_____

20 _____ •_____

_____

_____

20 _____ •_____

_____

_____

20 _____ •_____

_____

_____

_____

March

If you sit down, you will not be afraid; when you lie down, your sleep will be sweet.
Proverbs 3.24

How well are you sleeping at the moment?

20 ___ . _____

20 ___ . _____

20 ___ . _____

20 ___ . _____

20 ___ . _____

March

And let us consider how to provoke one another
to love and good deeds, not neglecting to meet
together . . . but encouraging one another.
Hebrews 10.24–25

In what way is going to church an
encouraging experience for you?

20 _____ •_____

_____

_____

20 _____ •_____

_____

_____

20 _____ •_____

_____

_____

20 _____ •_____

_____

_____

20 _____ •_____

_____

_____

_____

11

March

The woman said to Peter, 'You are not also one of this man's disciples, are you?' He said, 'I am not.'
John 18.17

Are there people in your life who would be surprised to know you are a Christian?

20 _____ •_____

20 _____ •_____

20 _____ •_____

20 _____ •_____

20 _____ •_____

March

So David reigned over all Israel; and he administered justice and equity to all his people.
1 Chronicles 18.14

12

How well do you think your government is governing?

20 _____ •_____

_____

_____

_____

20 _____ •_____

_____

_____

_____

20 _____ •_____

_____

_____

_____

20 _____ •_____

_____

_____

_____

20 _____ •_____

_____

_____

_____

13

March

'He will wipe every tear from their eyes. Death will be no more; mourning and crying and pain will be no more, for the first things have passed away.' *Revelation 21.4*

How do you imagine eternal life will be?

20 _____ •

20 _____ •

20 _____ •

20 _____ •

20 _____ •

March

So also the tongue is a small member,
yet it boasts of great exploits. How great
a forest is set ablaze by a small fire!
James 3.5

What circumstances make gossip more
of a temptation for you?

20 _____

20 _____

20 _____

20 _____

20 _____

15

March

Be gracious to me, O LORD, for I am
languishing; O LORD, heal me, for my
bones are shaking with terror.
Psalm 6.2

How have you learned to manage
(or live with) pain?

20 _____ •_____

_____

_____

_____

20 _____ •_____

_____

_____

_____

20 _____ •_____

_____

_____

_____

20 _____ •_____

_____

_____

_____

20 _____ •_____

_____

_____

_____

March

16

Let us know, let us press on to know the LORD;
   his appearing is as sure as the dawn;
   he will come to us like the showers.
   Hosea 6.3

Did the world look beautiful today?

20 ____ •_____

_____

_____

20 ____ •_____

_____

_____

20 ____ •_____

_____

_____

20 ____ •_____

_____

_____

20 ____ •_____

_____

_____

17

March

Finally, all of you, have unity of spirit, sympathy, love for one another, a tender heart, and a humble mind.
1 Peter 3.8

How closely does your church work with other churches in the area?

20 _____ •

20 _____ •

20 _____ •

20 _____ •

20 _____ •

March

When Jesus saw him lying there and knew that
he had been there a long time, he said to him,
'Do you want to be made well?'
John 5.6

Are you praying for anyone who is
chronically or terminally ill?

20 ____•_____

_____

_____

20 ____•_____

_____

_____

20 ____•_____

_____

_____

20 ____•_____

_____

_____

20 ____•_____

_____

_____

_____

19

March

The alien . . . shall be to you as the citizen
among you; you shall love the alien as yourself,
for you were aliens in the land of Egypt.
Leviticus 19.34

In the light of recent events, how
do you feel you should respond?

20 _____ •

20 _____ •

20 _____ •

20 _____ •

20 _____ •

March

20

We have not ceased praying for you and
asking that you may be ... fully pleasing to
him, as you bear fruit in every good work
and as you grow in the knowledge of God.
Colossians 1.9–10

Who do you pray will get to know God better?

20 _____ •_____

_____

_____

20 _____ •_____

_____

_____

20 _____ •_____

_____

_____

20 _____ •_____

_____

_____

20 _____ •_____

_____

_____

March

And taking the five loaves and the two fish, he looked up to heaven, and blessed and broke them, and gave them to the disciples to set before the crowd. *Luke 9.16*

When did you last enjoy a meal in great company?

20 _____ •

20 _____ •

20 _____ •

20 _____ •

20 _____ •

March

Deliver me from my enemies, O my God;
protect me from those who rise up
against me. *Psalm 59.1*

How do you cope when you think
someone doesn't like you?

20 _____ •

20 _____ •

20 _____ •

20 _____ •

20 _____ •

23

March

May [you] have the power to comprehend . . .
what is the breadth and length and height
and depth, and to know the love of Christ
that surpasses knowledge. *Ephesians 3.18*

Have you experienced a difficult day (or time)
that was suddenly transformed by God's love?

20 _____ •_____

_____

_____

20 _____ •_____

_____

_____

20 _____ •_____

_____

_____

20 _____ •_____

_____

_____

20 _____ •_____

_____

_____

March

24

[The king] cried out ... 'O Daniel, servant
of the living God, has your God whom
you faithfully serve been able to deliver
you from the lions?' *Daniel 6.20*

When was the last time you felt in
need of rescuing?

20 ____ •_____

_____

_____

20 ____ •_____

_____

_____

20 ____ •_____

_____

_____

20 ____ •_____

_____

_____

20 ____ •_____

_____

_____

_____

25

March

The angel said to her, 'The Holy Spirit
will come upon you, and the power of the
Most High will overshadow you . . . he
will be called Son of God.' *Luke 1.35*

Have you felt God calling you to undertake
something extraordinary this year?

20 ____ .

20 ____ .

20 ____ .

20 ____ .

20 ____ .

March

26

We destroy arguments and every proud
obstacle raised up against the knowledge of
God, and we take every thought captive
to obey Christ. *2 Corinthians 10.4–5*

When do you find it most difficult
to control your thoughts?

20 _____ •_____

_____

_____

_____

20 _____ •_____

_____

_____

_____

20 _____ •_____

_____

_____

_____

20 _____ •_____

_____

_____

_____

20 _____ •_____

_____

_____

_____

27

March

Jesus said to him, 'If you wish to be perfect, go, sell your possessions, and give the money to the poor, and you will have treasure in heaven.'
Matthew 19.21

What is your most treasured possession?

20 _____ •

20 _____ •

20 _____ •

20 _____ •

20 _____ •

March

28

For it was you who formed my inward parts;
you knit me together in my mother's womb.
Psalm 139.13

What do you like most about
your body – and least?

20 ____ •

20 ____ •

20 ____ •

20 ____ •

20 ____ •

29

March

If we confess our sins, he who is faithful
and just will forgive us our sins and
cleanse us from all unrighteousness.
1 John 1.9

What do you struggle to forgive yourself for?

20 _____ •_____

_____

_____

20 _____ •_____

_____

_____

20 _____ •_____

_____

_____

20 _____ •_____

_____

_____

20 _____ •_____

_____

_____

March

30

Some friends play at friendship but a true
friend sticks closer than one's nearest kin.
Proverbs 18.24

How do you keep in touch with friends
who live far away?

20 ____ •_____

_____

_____

_____

20 ____ •_____

_____

_____

_____

20 ____ •_____

_____

_____

_____

20 ____ •_____

_____

_____

_____

20 ____ •_____

_____

_____

_____

31

March

'I give you a new commandment, that you love one another ... By this everyone will know that you are my disciples, if you have love for one another.' *John 13.34–35*

What have you done today that's shown your love for someone?

20 ___ •

20 ___ •

20 ___ •

20 ___ •

20 ___ •

April

1

Conduct yourselves wisely towards outsiders,
making the most of the time.
Colossians 4.5

What is one useful thing you might
take up in the next month?

20 _____ •_____

_____

20 _____ •_____

_____

20 _____ •_____

_____

20 _____ •_____

_____

20 _____ •_____

_____

April

You say, 'How have we despised your name?'
By offering polluted food on my altar.
Malachi 1.6–7

Do you feel your church is viewed
positively in the local community?

20 ___ •

20 ___ •

20 ___ •

20 ___ •

20 ___ •

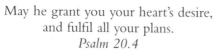 *April*

May he grant you your heart's desire,
and fulfil all your plans.
Psalm 20.4

Have you something relaxing and enjoyable
to look forward to this week?

20 ___ •_____

_____

_____

20 ___ •_____

_____

_____

20 ___ •_____

_____

_____

20 ___ •_____

_____

_____

20 ___ •_____

_____

_____

April

Of course, there is great gain in godliness combined with contentment.
1 Timothy 6.6

What would you like people to
remember you for?

20 _____ •

20 _____ •

20 _____ •

20 _____ •

20 _____ •

April

When I called, no one answered, when I spoke,
they did not listen; but they did what was evil in
my sight, and chose what did not please me.
Isaiah 66.4

When did you last feel let down – or let
down someone else?

20 _____ •_____

_____

_____

_____

20 _____ •_____

_____

_____

_____

20 _____ •_____

_____

_____

_____

20 _____ •_____

_____

_____

_____

20 _____ •_____

_____

_____

_____

6

April

But if God so clothes the grass of the field, which is alive today and tomorrow is thrown into the oven, how much more will he clothe you.
Luke 12.28

What things have you worried about today that you didn't really need to?

20 _____ •

20 _____ •

20 _____ •

20 _____ •

20 _____ •

April

Therefore confess your sins to one another, and pray
for one another, so that you may be healed. The
prayer of the righteous is powerful and effective.
James 5.16

Who have you confessed to recently – Christian
friends, a spiritual director or minister?

20 _____ •_____

_____

_____

20 _____ •_____

_____

_____

20 _____ •_____

_____

_____

20 _____ •_____

_____

_____

20 _____ •_____

_____

_____

_____

April

And Ruth the Moabite said to Naomi, 'Let me
go to the field and glean among the ears of
grain, behind someone in whose sight
I may find favour.' *Ruth 2.2*

When did you last feel someone
was protecting you?

20 ____ •_____

_____

_____

20 ____ •_____

_____

_____

20 ____ •_____

_____

_____

20 ____ •_____

_____

_____

20 ____ •_____

_____

_____

April

9

Remember your leaders, those who spoke the
word of God to you; consider the outcome of
their way of life, and imitate their faith.
Hebrews 13.7

What are the qualities you admire
in your church leaders?

20 _____ •_____

_____

_____

20 _____ •_____

_____

_____

20 _____ •_____

_____

_____

20 _____ •_____

_____

_____

20 _____ •_____

_____

_____

_____

10

April

Just as [the Gospel] is bearing fruit and
growing in the whole world, so it has
been bearing fruit among yourselves.
Colossians 1.6

Have you Christian friends in other
countries who need your prayers?

20 _____ •_____

_____

_____

20 _____ •_____

_____

_____

20 _____ •_____

_____

_____

20 _____ •_____

_____

_____

20 _____ •_____

_____

_____

_____

April

11

When the righteous cry for help, the LORD hears,
and rescues them from all their troubles.
Psalm 34.17

What trouble would you like to bring to God?

20 ____ • _____

_____

_____

20 ____ • _____

_____

_____

20 ____ • _____

_____

_____

20 ____ • _____

_____

_____

20 ____ • _____

_____

_____

12

April

Daniel . . . continued . . . to get down
on his knees three times a day to pray
to his God and praise him.
Daniel 6.10

Have any distractions hindered
you from praying today?

20 _____ •_____

_____

_____

20 _____ •_____

_____

_____

20 _____ •_____

_____

_____

20 _____ •_____

_____

_____

20 _____ •_____

_____

_____

_____

April

Do nothing from selfish ambition or
conceit, but in humility regard others
as better than yourselves.
Philippians 2.3

Who do you find yourself criticizing?
Why might this be?

20 ____•_____

20 ____•_____

20 ____•_____

20 ____•_____

20 ____•_____

14

April

When Jesus came to the place, he looked up and said to him, 'Zacchaeus, hurry and come down; for I must stay at your house today.'
Luke 19.5

How have you been surprised by God recently?

20 _____ •_____

20 _____ •_____

20 _____ •_____

20 _____ •_____

20 _____ •_____

April

15

When I am afraid, I put my trust in you.
In God, whose word I praise, in God I trust;
I am not afraid; what can flesh do to me?
Psalm 56.3–4

What causes you to feel anxious?

20 ____ •_____

_____

_____

20 ____ •_____

_____

_____

20 ____ •_____

_____

_____

20 ____ •_____

_____

_____

20 ____ •_____

_____

_____

16

April

Have nothing to do with stupid and senseless controversies; you know that they breed quarrels.
2 Timothy 2.23

When was the last time you got involved in a 'stupid and senseless' argument?

20 _____ •

20 _____ •

20 _____ •

20 _____ •

20 _____ •

April

17

Your proud heart has deceived you,
you . . . whose dwelling is in the heights.
You say in your heart, 'Who will bring
me down to the ground?' *Obadiah 3*

How do you balance sensible
provision with relying on God?

20 _____ •_____

_____

_____

20 _____ •_____

_____

_____

20 _____ •_____

_____

_____

20 _____ •_____

_____

_____

20 _____ •_____

_____

_____

_____

18

April

The only thing that counts is
faith working through love.
Galatians 5.6

How did you express love to someone today?

20 ____ •_____

_____

_____

20 ____ •_____

_____

_____

20 ____ •_____

_____

_____

20 ____ •_____

_____

_____

20 ____ •_____

_____

_____

April

19

'I am the good shepherd. I know my own and my own know me, just as the Father knows me and I know the Father. And I lay down my life for the sheep.' *John 10.14–15*

What cares would you like to leave with Jesus right now?

20 _____ •_____

_____

_____

20 _____ •_____

_____

_____

20 _____ •_____

_____

_____

20 _____ •_____

_____

_____

20 _____ •_____

_____

_____

_____

20

April

Then he said, 'Come no closer! Remove the sandals from your feet, for the place on which you are standing is holy ground.'
Exodus 3.5

Where for you is 'holy ground'?

20 _____ •

20 _____ •

20 _____ •

20 _____ •

20 _____ •

April

And whatever you do, in word or deed,
do everything in the name of the Lord Jesus,
giving thanks to God the Father through him.
Colossians 3.17

Do you think your words or your actions
tend to speak louder to others?

20 _____•_____

_____

_____

20 _____•_____

_____

_____

20 _____•_____

_____

_____

20 _____•_____

_____

_____

20 _____•_____

_____

_____

22

April

The LORD is my shepherd, I shall not want.
He makes me lie down in green pastures;
he leads me beside still waters.
Psalm 23.1–2

When was the last time you
enjoyed 'still waters'?

20 _____ •_____

_____

_____

20 _____ •_____

_____

_____

20 _____ •_____

_____

_____

20 _____ •_____

_____

_____

20 _____ •_____

_____

_____

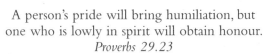

April

A person's pride will bring humiliation, but
one who is lowly in spirit will obtain honour.
Proverbs 29.23

Does any well-known person come
to mind after reading this verse?

20 _____ ● _____

_____

_____

20 _____ ● _____

_____

_____

20 _____ ● _____

_____

_____

20 _____ ● _____

_____

_____

20 _____ ● _____

_____

_____

24

April

To you then who believe, he is precious;
but for those who do not believe, 'The
stone that the builders rejected has become
the very head of the corner.' *1 Peter 2.7*

Have you felt rejected recently?
Does this verse ease the pain?

20 ____ •_____

_____

_____

20 ____ •_____

_____

_____

20 ____ •_____

_____

_____

20 ____ •_____

_____

_____

20 ____ •_____

_____

_____

April

25

But when you give alms, do not let your left
hand know what your right hand is doing.
Matthew 6.3

Which charity or charities do you
support on a regular basis?

20 ____ •

20 ____ •

20 ____ •

20 ____ •

20 ____ •

26

April

For thus says the LORD to the house
of Israel: Seek me and live.
Amos 5.4

Where do you look for God?

20 _____ • _____

_____

_____

20 _____ • _____

_____

_____

20 _____ • _____

_____

_____

20 _____ • _____

_____

_____

20 _____ • _____

_____

_____

_____

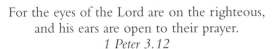

April

27

For the eyes of the Lord are on the righteous,
and his ears are open to their prayer.
1 Peter 3.12

Who do you trust to pray for you faithfully?

20 _____ ● _____

_____

_____

20 _____ ● _____

_____

_____

20 _____ ● _____

_____

_____

20 _____ ● _____

_____

_____

20 _____ ● _____

_____

_____

April

O LORD, how manifold are your works!
In wisdom you have made them all;
the earth is full of your creatures.
Psalm 104.24

Do you feel you've become wiser (perhaps
through particular experiences) in the past year?

20 _____ •_____

20 _____ •_____

20 _____ •_____

20 _____ •_____

20 _____ •_____

April

29

But you are a God ready to forgive, gracious
and merciful, slow to anger and abounding in
steadfast love, and you did not forsake them.
Nehemiah 9.17

What did you ask God to forgive today?

20 ____ •_____

_____

_____

20 ____ •_____

_____

_____

20 ____ •_____

_____

_____

20 ____ •_____

_____

_____

20 ____ •_____

_____

_____

30

April

Be careful then how you live, not as unwise
people but as wise, making the most of
the time, because the days are evil.
Ephesians 5.15–16

What are the greatest priorities
in your life at the moment?

20 ____ •_____
_____
_____

20 ____ •_____
_____
_____

20 ____ •_____
_____
_____

20 ____ •_____
_____
_____

20 ____ •_____
_____
_____

May

Then they told what had happened on the
road, and how he had been made known
to them in the breaking of the bread.
Luke 24.35

Who are the people you have
seen Jesus in recently?

20 ____ •_____

_____

_____

20 ____ •_____

_____

_____

20 ____ •_____

_____

_____

20 ____ •_____

_____

_____

20 ____ •_____

_____

_____

_____

May

But Hannah answered . . . 'Do not regard
your servant as a worthless woman, for I have
been speaking out of my great anxiety and
vexation all this time.' *1 Samuel 1.15–16*

Is there someone you feel you may
have misjudged?

20 ___ •_____

_____

_____

20 ___ •_____

_____

_____

20 ___ •_____

_____

_____

20 ___ •_____

_____

_____

20 ___ •_____

_____

_____

May

3

See what love the Father has given us,
that we should be called children of God;
and that is what we are.
1 John 3.1

When were you conscious today of
God's loving presence?

20 _____ •

20 _____ •

20 _____ •

20 _____ •

20 _____ •

4

May

Now faith is the assurance of things hoped for, the conviction of things not seen.
Hebrews 11.1

What is testing or stretching your faith at the moment?

20 ___ •

20 ___ •

20 ___ •

20 ___ •

20 ___ •

May

You prepare a table before me in the
presence of my enemies; you anoint
my head with oil; my cup overflows.
Psalm 23.5

In what way is your cup 'overflowing'?

20 _____•_____

20 _____•_____

20 _____•_____

20 _____•_____

20 _____•_____

6

May

Do not be deceived; God is not mocked,
for you reap whatever you sow.
Galatians 6.7

What good decisions have you made lately?

20 _____ •_____

_____

_____

20 _____ •_____

_____

_____

20 _____ •_____

_____

_____

20 _____ •_____

_____

_____

20 _____ •_____

_____

_____

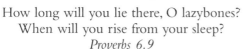 

May 7

How long will you lie there, O lazybones?
When will you rise from your sleep?
Proverbs 6.9

How energetic have you been feeling today?
What have you accomplished?

20 _____ •_____

_____

_____

20 _____ •_____

_____

_____

20 _____ •_____

_____

_____

20 _____ •_____

_____

_____

20 _____ •_____

_____

_____

 **8**

May

And having been warned in a dream not to return to Herod, they left for their own country by another road. *Matthew 2.12*

How does God speak to you – through the Bible, nature, the words of others, dreams, or by some other means?

20 ____ •

20 ____ •

20 ____ •

20 ____ •

20 ____ •

May

And hear the plea of your servant and of your
people Israel, when they pray towards this place;
may you hear from heaven your dwelling place;
hear and forgive. *2 Chronicles 6.21*

What difficulties prompted you to turn to
God in prayer today?

20 _____ •

20 _____ •

20 _____ •

20 _____ •

20 _____ •

10

May

One thing more – prepare a guest room
for me, for I am hoping through your
prayers to be restored to you.
Philemon 22

Which biblical figure would you enjoy
entertaining in your home?

20 _____ •_____

_____

_____

20 _____ •_____

_____

_____

20 _____ •_____

_____

_____

20 _____ •_____

_____

_____

20 _____ •_____

_____

_____

_____

May

11

Deal bountifully with your servant, so that I may
live and observe your word. Open my eyes, so that
I may behold wondrous things out of your law.
Psalm 119.17–18

Is there a spiritual writer/speaker who
has given you a fresh perspective?

20 ____ •_____

_____

_____

20 ____ •_____

_____

_____

20 ____ •_____

_____

_____

20 ____ •_____

_____

_____

20 ____ •_____

_____

_____

May

And a harvest of righteousness is sown in
peace for those who make peace.
James 3.18

In which situations could you
be more of a peacemaker?

20 _____ •_____

_____

_____

20 _____ •_____

_____

_____

20 _____ •_____

_____

_____

20 _____ •_____

_____

_____

20 _____ •_____

_____

_____

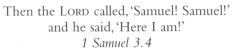

May

13

Then the LORD called, 'Samuel! Samuel!'
and he said, 'Here I am!'
1 Samuel 3.4

On a scale of 1–5, how available have
you been to God today?

20 ____ •_____

_____

_____

20 ____ •_____

_____

_____

20 ____ •_____

_____

_____

20 ____ •_____

_____

_____

20 ____ •_____

_____

_____

_____

14

May

[The woman] declared in the presence of
all the people why she had touched him,
and how she had been immediately healed.
Luke 8.47

How do you cope when God doesn't appear
to be healing someone despite much prayer?

20 _____ •_____

_____

_____

20 _____ •_____

_____

_____

20 _____ •_____

_____

_____

20 _____ •_____

_____

_____

20 _____ •_____

_____

_____

May

15

Conduct yourselves honourably among the Gentiles, so that . . . they may see your honourable deeds and glorify God when he comes to judge. *1 Peter 2.12*

Did you do anything today that was an encouragement to someone?

20 _____ •_____

20 _____ •_____

20 _____ •_____

20 _____ •_____

20 _____ •_____

16

May

Wash yourselves; make yourselves clean;
remove the evil of your doings from
before my eyes; cease to do evil.
Isaiah 1.16

When did you last experience wickedness?

20 ___ •

20 ___ •

20 ___ •

20 ___ •

20 ___ •

May

17

Now to him who by the power at work within
us is able to accomplish abundantly far more
than all we can ask or imagine.
Ephesians 3.20

Does this verse encourage you to pray
for a particular issue?

20 _____ •_____

_____

_____

20 _____ •_____

_____

_____

20 _____ •_____

_____

_____

20 _____ •_____

_____

_____

20 _____ •_____

_____

_____

_____

18

May

You will say to the LORD, 'My refuge and
my fortress; my God, in whom I trust.'
Psalm 91.2

Did anything happen today that reassured
you how much God cares for you?

20 _____ •

20 _____ •

20 _____ •

20 _____ •

20 _____ •

May

19

But whenever you pray, go into your
room and shut the door and pray to your
Father who is in secret; and your Father
who sees in secret will reward you.
Matthew 6.6

Where is your special place to pray?

20 _____

20 _____

20 _____

20 _____

20 _____

20

May

Do all things without murmuring and
arguing, so that you may be blameless and
innocent, children of God . . . in which
you shine like stars in the world.
Philippians 2.14–15

Who 'shone like a star' for you today?

20 _____ •_____

_____

_____

20 _____ •_____

_____

_____

20 _____ •_____

_____

_____

20 _____ •_____

_____

_____

20 _____ •_____

_____

_____

_____

May

21

Then everyone who calls on the name
of the LORD shall be saved.
Joel 2.32

Who are the people you long
to know God's love?

20 _____ •_____

_____

_____

20 _____ •_____

_____

_____

20 _____ •_____

_____

_____

20 _____ •_____

_____

_____

20 _____ •_____

_____

_____

_____

22

May

Now there are varieties of gifts, but
the same Spirit; and there are varieties
of services, but the same Lord.
1 Corinthians 12.4–5

What do you think are your spiritual gifts?

20 ____ •

20 ____ •

20 ____ •

20 ____ •

20 ____ •

May

23

A new heart I will give you, and a new spirit
I will put within you; and I will remove from
your body the heart of stone and give
you a heart of flesh. *Ezekiel 36.26*

Have you felt your spirits lifted by
some event today?

20 _____ •_____

_____

_____

20 _____ •_____

_____

_____

20 _____ •_____

_____

_____

20 _____ •_____

_____

_____

20 _____ •_____

_____

_____

_____

24

May

The grace of God has appeared . . . training us to renounce impiety and worldly passions, and in the present age to live lives that are self-controlled, upright, and godly. *Titus 2.12*

What 'worldly passion' is tempting you at the moment?

20 ___ •

20 ___ •

20 ___ •

20 ___ •

20 ___ •

May

25

Let them thank the LORD for his steadfast love, for his wonderful works to humankind. For he satisfies the thirsty, and the hungry he fills with good things. *Psalm 107.8–9*

How have you learned from your encounters with people in need?

20 _____ •_____

20 _____ •_____

20 _____ •_____

20 _____ •_____

20 _____ •_____

26

May

During the night Paul had a vision:
there stood a man of Macedonia pleading
with him and saying, 'Come over to
Macedonia and help us.' *Acts 16.9*

Has a door opened for you recently?

20 _____ •_____

_____

_____

20 _____ •_____

_____

_____

20 _____ •_____

_____

_____

20 _____ •_____

_____

_____

20 _____ •_____

_____

_____

May

27

You must make every effort to support
your faith with goodness . . . and endurance
with godliness, and godliness with mutual
affection, and mutual affection with love.
2 Peter 1.5–7

Where did you experience goodness today?

20 ____ •_____

_____

_____

20 ____ •_____

_____

_____

20 ____ •_____

_____

_____

20 ____ •_____

_____

_____

20 ____ •_____

_____

_____

_____

28

May

Your eyes are too pure to behold evil . . .
why do you look on the treacherous, and are
silent when the wicked swallow those more
righteous than they? *Habakkuk 1.13*

What question would you like to ask God
about the world we live in?

20 _____ •

20 _____ •

20 _____ •

20 _____ •

20 _____ •

May

'I am the resurrection and the life. Those who believe in me, even though they die, will live, and everyone who lives and believes in me will never die.' *John 11.25–26*

Who do you know who might be responsive to this message just now?

20 _____ •_____

_____

_____

20 _____ •_____

_____

_____

20 _____ •_____

_____

_____

20 _____ •_____

_____

_____

20 _____ •_____

_____

_____

_____

30

May

Are any among you suffering?
They should pray. Are any cheerful?
They should sing songs of praise.
James 5.13

Who do you know who is suffering?

20 _____ •_____

_____

_____

20 _____ •_____

_____

_____

20 _____ •_____

_____

_____

20 _____ •_____

_____

_____

20 _____ •_____

_____

_____

May

In his hand are the depths of the earth; the heights of the mountains are his also.
Psalm 95.4

If you could travel to anywhere in the world, where would you go?

20 _____ •_____

_____

_____

20 _____ •_____

_____

_____

20 _____ •_____

_____

_____

20 _____ •_____

_____

_____

20 _____ •_____

_____

_____

June

Be kind to one another, tender-hearted, forgiving
one another, as God in Christ has forgiven you.
Ephesians 4.32

Who were you kind to today?

20 _____ • _____

_____

_____

20 _____ • _____

_____

_____

20 _____ • _____

_____

_____

20 _____ • _____

_____

_____

20 _____ • _____

_____

_____

 *June*

But Sarah denied, saying, 'I did not laugh'; for she
was afraid. He said, 'Oh yes, you did laugh.'
Genesis 18.15

When was the last time you lied?
Do you think the lie was justified?

20 _____ •_____

_____

_____

_____

20 _____ •_____

_____

_____

_____

20 _____ •_____

_____

_____

_____

20 _____ •_____

_____

_____

_____

20 _____ •_____

_____

_____

_____

3

June

All scripture is inspired by God and is useful
for teaching, for reproof, for correction, and
for training in righteousness.
2 Timothy 3.16

Which books of the Bible have you
never read (or not for a long time!)?

20 ____ •_____

_____

_____

20 ____ •_____

_____

_____

20 ____ •_____

_____

_____

20 ____ •_____

_____

_____

20 ____ •_____

_____

_____

_____

June

Praise the LORD! Praise, O servants of the LORD;
praise the name of the LORD. Blessed be the name
of the LORD from this time on and for evermore.
Psalm 113.1–2

What are your three favourite
ways of praising God?

20 _____ •_____

_____

_____

20 _____ •_____

_____

_____

20 _____ •_____

_____

_____

20 _____ •_____

_____

_____

20 _____ •_____

_____

_____

5

June

For we are what he has made us, created in
Christ Jesus for good works, which God prepared
beforehand to be our way of life.
Ephesians 2.10

Can you see how God has prepared the
way for you in a particular situation?

20 _____ •_____

_____

_____

20 _____ •_____

_____

_____

20 _____ •_____

_____

_____

20 _____ •_____

_____

_____

20 _____ •_____

_____

_____

June

6

Yet, O LORD, you are our Father;
we are the clay, and you are our potter;
we are all the work of your hand.
Isaiah 64.8

Are there any ways you are hoping
God will change you?

20 _____ •_____
_____
_____

20 _____ •_____
_____
_____

20 _____ •_____
_____
_____

20 _____ •_____
_____
_____

20 _____ •_____
_____
_____

7

June

They went to him . . . shouting, 'Master,
Master, we are perishing!' And he woke up
and rebuked the wind and the raging waves;
they ceased, and there was a calm.
Luke 8.24

What storm in your life would you like calmed

20 _____ ●_____

20 _____ ●_____

20 _____ ●_____

20 _____ ●_____

20 _____ ●_____

June

Do not love the world or the things in
the world. The love of the Father is not
in those who love the world.
1 John 2.15

What is one way in which this
verse challenges you?

20 _____ •_____

_____

_____

20 _____ •_____

_____

_____

20 _____ •_____

_____

_____

20 _____ •_____

_____

_____

20 _____ •_____

_____

_____

June

I remember the days of old, I think about all your
deeds, I meditate on the works of your hands.
Psalm 143.5

What is your happiest memory?

20 _____.

20 _____.

20 _____.

20 _____.

20 _____.

June

Martha . . . asked, 'Lord, do you not care that
my sister has left me to do all the work by
myself? Tell her then to help me.'
Luke 10.40

Are you more like Martha or
her sister Mary? In what ways?

20 _____ •_____

_____

_____

20 _____ •_____

_____

_____

20 _____ •_____

_____

_____

20 _____ •_____

_____

_____

20 _____ •_____

_____

_____

_____

11

June

But each of us was given grace according
to the measure of Christ's gift.
Ephesians 4.7

Is there anyone you know who is finding it
hard to accept Jesus' unconditional love?

20 _____ •_____

_____

_____

20 _____ •_____

_____

_____

20 _____ •_____

_____

_____

20 _____ •_____

_____

_____

20 _____ •_____

_____

_____

June

The conspirators came and found Daniel
praying and seeking mercy before his God.
Daniel 6.11

Have you been in a difficult situation
recently? How did you respond?

20 ____ •_____

_____

_____

20 ____ •_____

_____

_____

20 ____ •_____

_____

_____

20 ____ •_____

_____

_____

20 ____ •_____

_____

_____

13

June

Those who do not love a brother or
sister whom they have seen, cannot
love God whom they have not seen.
1 John 4.20

Do you have a difficult relationship with
someone that you might pray about?

20 _____ •_____

_____

_____

_____

20 _____ •_____

_____

_____

_____

20 _____ •_____

_____

_____

_____

20 _____ •_____

_____

_____

_____

20 _____ •_____

_____

_____

_____

June

Take delight in the LORD, and he will
give you the desires of your heart.
Psalm 37.4

What are the desires of your heart?

20 _____ •_____

_____

_____

20 _____ •_____

_____

_____

20 _____ •_____

_____

_____

20 _____ •_____

_____

_____

20 _____ •_____

_____

_____

15

June

'Come to me, all you that are weary and are carrying heavy burdens, and I will give you rest.'
Matthew 11.28

What is weighing you down at the moment?

20 _____ •_____

_____

_____

20 _____ •_____

_____

_____

20 _____ •_____

_____

_____

20 _____ •_____

_____

_____

20 _____ •_____

_____

_____

June

16

Let each of you look not to your own
interests, but to the interests of others.
Philippians 2.4

How are you involved in your community?

20 ___ •_____

_____

_____

20 ___ •_____

_____

_____

20 ___ •_____

_____

_____

20 ___ •_____

_____

_____

20 ___ •_____

_____

_____

_____

17

June

Do not fear, for I am with you, do not be
afraid, for I am your God; I will strengthen you,
I will help you, I will uphold you with
my victorious right hand.
Isaiah 41.10

How has God drawn near to you today?

20 _____ •_____

_____

_____

20 _____ •_____

_____

_____

20 _____ •_____

_____

_____

20 _____ •_____

_____

_____

20 _____ •_____

_____

_____

June 18

Indeed, the word of God is living
and active, sharper than any two-edged
sword . . . it is able to judge the thoughts
and intentions of the heart. *Hebrews 4.12*

Which Bible passage(s) do you most
often turn to?

20 ___ •_____

_____

_____

20 ___ •_____

_____

_____

20 ___ •_____

_____

_____

20 ___ •_____

_____

_____

20 ___ •_____

_____

_____

_____

19

June

Although I have much to write to you . . . instead I hope to come to you and talk with you face to face, so that our joy may be complete.
2 John 12

Who did you last really enjoy seeing?

20 _____ • _____
_____
_____

20 _____ • _____
_____
_____

20 _____ • _____
_____
_____

20 _____ • _____
_____
_____

20 _____ • _____
_____
_____

June

O God, do not keep silence; do not hold
your peace or be still, O God!
Psalm 83.1

Which of your prayers do you most
long to be answered?

20 _____•_____

_____

_____

20 _____•_____

_____

_____

20 _____•_____

_____

_____

20 _____•_____

_____

_____

20 _____•_____

_____

_____

_____

21 June

'No one can serve two masters . . .
You cannot serve God and wealth.'
Matthew 6.24

How well are you managing your money?

20 _____ •_____

_____

_____

20 _____ •_____

_____

_____

20 _____ •_____

_____

_____

20 _____ •_____

_____

_____

20 _____ •_____

_____

_____

_____

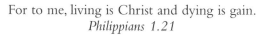*June*

For to me, living is Christ and dying is gain.
Philippians 1.21

Have you been in a situation this year that has
forced you to contemplate your mortality?
How did you respond?

20 _____ •_____

_____

_____

20 _____ •_____

_____

_____

_____

20 _____ •_____

_____

_____

_____

20 _____ •_____

_____

_____

_____

20 _____ •_____

_____

_____

_____

Elijah said to Elisha, 'Stay here; for the
LORD has sent me as far as Bethel.' But Elisha
said, '. . . I will not leave you.' So they
went down to Bethel. *2 Kings 2.2*

In what ways are you a good friend?

20 _____ •_____

_____

_____

20 _____ •_____

_____

_____

20 _____ •_____

_____

_____

20 _____ •_____

_____

_____

20 _____ •_____

_____

_____

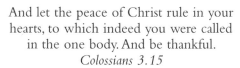

June

And let the peace of Christ rule in your
hearts, to which indeed you were called
in the one body. And be thankful.
Colossians 3.15

When did you last feel 'peace
beyond understanding'?

20 ____ •_____

_____

_____

_____

20 ____ •_____

_____

_____

_____

20 ____ •_____

_____

_____

_____

20 ____ •_____

_____

_____

_____

20 ____ •_____

_____

_____

_____

_____

25

June

Zacchaeus . . . said to the Lord, 'Look, half of my possessions, Lord, I will give to the poor; and if I have defrauded anyone of anything, I will pay back four times as much.' *Luke 19.8*

Is there someone in your church community you need to forgive?

20 _____ •

20 _____ •

20 _____ •

20 _____ •

20 _____ •

June

Weeping may linger for the night,
but joy comes with the morning.
Psalm 30.5

How do you respond to this verse?

20 _____ •_____

_____

_____

20 _____ •_____

_____

_____

20 _____ •_____

_____

_____

20 _____ •_____

_____

_____

20 _____ •_____

_____

_____

_____

27

June

And it is no longer I who live, but it is
Christ who lives in me . . . who loved
me and gave himself for me.
Galatians 2.20

How can you perceive Jesus living in you?

20 ____ • _____

_____

_____

20 ____ • _____

_____

_____

20 ____ • _____

_____

_____

20 ____ • _____

_____

_____

20 ____ • _____

_____

_____

June

But Ruth said, 'Do not press me to leave you . . . Where you go, I will go . . . your people shall be my people, and your God my God.' *Ruth 1.16*

Who are the people in your life that you most care about?

20 ____ •_____

_____

_____

_____

20 ____ •_____

_____

_____

_____

20 ____ •_____

_____

_____

_____

20 ____ •_____

_____

_____

_____

20 ____ •_____

_____

_____

_____

June

Lead a life ... with all humility and gentleness, with patience, bearing with one another in love. *Ephesians 4.2*

Is there anyone who is trying your patience at the moment?

20 _____ •_____

20 _____ •_____

20 _____ •_____

20 _____ •_____

20 _____ •_____

June

All things came into being through him, and
without him not one thing came into being.
John 1.3

What, for you, is one of the most surprising
aspects of God's creation?

20 _____ •

20 _____ •

20 _____ •

20 _____ •

20 _____ •

1

July

A friend loves at all times, and kinsfolk are born to share adversity.
Proverbs 17.17

What could you do for a friend this week to show you value that friend?

20 _____ ●_____

_____

_____

20 _____ ●_____

_____

_____

20 _____ ●_____

_____

_____

20 _____ ●_____

_____

_____

20 _____ ●_____

_____

_____

July

He who rescued us from so deadly a peril will
continue to rescue us; on him we have set
our hope that he will rescue us again.
2 Corinthians 1.10

When did you last experience
Christ coming to your rescue?

20 _____ •_____

_____

_____

_____

20 _____ •_____

_____

_____

_____

20 _____ •_____

_____

_____

_____

20 _____ •_____

_____

_____

_____

20 _____ •_____

_____

_____

_____

3

July

Have mercy on me, O God, according
to your steadfast love; according to your
abundant mercy blot out my transgressions.
Psalm 51.1

Do you need to let go of something in
your life that isn't doing you good?

20 _____ •_____
_____
_____
_____

20 _____ •_____
_____
_____
_____

20 _____ •_____
_____
_____
_____

20 _____ •_____
_____
_____
_____

20 _____ •_____
_____
_____
_____

July

Then Jesus told his disciples, 'If any want to
become my followers, let them deny themselves
and take up their cross and follow me.'
Matthew 16.24

When was the last time you stepped
out of your comfort zone?

20 ___ •_____

_____

_____

20 ___ •_____

_____

_____

20 ___ •_____

_____

_____

20 ___ •_____

_____

_____

20 ___ •_____

_____

_____

5

July

By contrast, the fruit of the Spirit is love, joy, peace, patience, kindness, generosity, faithfulness, gentleness, and self-control. There is no law against such things. *Galatians 5.22–23*

How do you think others see God working in your life?

20 _____ •

20 _____ •

20 _____ •

20 _____ •

20 _____ •

July

But now thus says the LORD, he who created
you . . . O Israel: Do not fear, for I have
redeemed you; I have called you by
name, you are mine. *Isaiah 43.1*

Imagine God gently speaking your name.
How do your mind and heart respond?

20 ___ •_____

_____

_____

_____

20 ___ •_____

_____

_____

_____

20 ___ •_____

_____

_____

_____

20 ___ •_____

_____

_____

_____

20 ___ •_____

_____

_____

_____

7

July

Since we have these promises, beloved, let us cleanse ourselves from every defilement of body and of spirit, making holiness perfect in the fear of God. *2 Corinthians 7.1*

What good habit have you developed in the past year?

20 _____ •

20 _____ •

20 _____ •

20 _____ •

20 _____ •

July

When Jesus saw her weeping . . . he was
greatly disturbed in spirit and deeply moved.
He said, 'Where have you laid him?'
They said to him, 'Lord, come and see.'
John 11.33–34

Who are you mourning?

20 _____ •_____

_____

_____

20 _____ •_____

_____

_____

20 _____ •_____

_____

_____

20 _____ •_____

_____

_____

20 _____ •_____

_____

_____

_____

9

July

Be strong and bold; have no fear or dread of them,
because it is the LORD your God who goes with
you; he will not fail you or forsake you.
Deuteronomy 31.6

What risky thing do you think
God would love you to tackle?

20 _____ •

20 _____ •

20 _____ •

20 _____ •

20 _____ •

July

In our prayers for you we always thank God,
the Father of our Lord Jesus Christ.
Colossians 1.3

Who would you especially like to
thank God for today?

20 _____ •_____

_____

_____

_____

20 _____ •_____

_____

_____

_____

20 _____ •_____

_____

_____

_____

20 _____ •_____

_____

_____

_____

20 _____ •_____

_____

_____

_____

The heavens are telling the glory of God;
and the firmament proclaims his handiwork.
Psalm 19.1

What is the most beautiful
sight you've seen this year?

20 _____ •

20 _____ •

20 _____ •

20 _____ •

20 _____ •

July

12

And if we know that he hears us in
whatever we ask, we know that we have
obtained the requests made of him.
1 John 5.15

Who have you been praying for today?

20 ____ •_____

_____

_____

20 ____ •_____

_____

_____

20 ____ •_____

_____

_____

20 ____ •_____

_____

_____

20 ____ •_____

_____

_____

13

July

Oh, rebellious children, says the LORD, who
carry out a plan, but not mine . . . who set out
to go down to Egypt without asking for
my counsel. *Isaiah 30.1–2*

How do you involve God when
making big decisions?

20 _____ • _____
_____
_____

20 _____ • _____
_____
_____

20 _____ • _____
_____
_____

20 _____ • _____
_____
_____

20 _____ • _____
_____
_____
_____

July

14

Then Jesus said to the Jews who had
believed in him, 'If you continue in my
word, you are truly my disciples.'
John 8.31

What does it mean to you to be
a disciple of Jesus?

20 _____ •_____

20 _____ •_____

20 _____ •_____

20 _____ •_____

20 _____ •_____

Give thanks in all circumstances; for this is
the will of God in Christ Jesus for you.
1 Thessalonians 5.18

Has this verse altered your perspective
in a recent difficulty?

20 _____ •

20 _____ •

20 _____ •

20 _____ •

20 _____ •

July

16

See, the LORD's hand is not too short to save,
nor his ear too dull to hear.
Isaiah 59.1

God hears us: how do you listen out for him?

20 ____ •_____

20 ____ •_____

20 ____ •_____

20 ____ •_____

20 ____ •_____

17

July

Therefore . . . let us also lay aside every weight and the sin that clings so closely, and let us run with perseverance the race that is set before us.
Hebrews 12.1

What are you having to persevere with at the moment?

20 ___ •_____

_____

_____

20 ___ •_____

_____

_____

20 ___ •_____

_____

_____

20 ___ •_____

_____

_____

20 ___ •_____

_____

_____

July

18

For God did not give us a spirit
of cowardice, but rather a spirit of power
and of love and of self-discipline.
2 Timothy 1.7

Have you been more of an
extrovert or introvert today?

20 _____ •_____

_____

_____

20 _____ •_____

_____

_____

20 _____ •_____

_____

_____

20 _____ •_____

_____

_____

20 _____ •_____

_____

_____

_____

19

July

I will instruct you and teach you
the way you should go; I will
counsel you with my eye upon you.
Psalm 32.8

What temptation do you find it hard to resist?

20 _____ •_____

_____

_____

20 _____ •_____

_____

_____

20 _____ •_____

_____

_____

20 _____ •_____

_____

_____

20 _____ •_____

_____

_____

_____

July

Then Jesus entered the temple and drove
out all who were selling and buying . . .
[overturning] the tables of the
money-changers. *Matthew 21.12*

How do you find yourself responding to
the decisiveness and drama of Jesus' actions?

20 _____ •_____

_____

_____

_____

20 _____ •_____

_____

_____

_____

20 _____ •_____

_____

_____

_____

20 _____ •_____

_____

_____

_____

20 _____ •_____

_____

_____

_____

21

July

For the love of God is this, that
we obey his commandments. And his
commandments are not burdensome.
1 John 5.3

What did you do for someone today
because you love him/her?

20 _____ •_____

_____

_____

20 _____ •_____

_____

_____

20 _____ •_____

_____

_____

20 _____ •_____

_____

_____

20 _____ •_____

_____

_____

Then I considered all that my hands had done and the toil I had spent in doing it . . . all was vanity . . . and there was nothing to be gained under the sun. *Ecclesiastes 2.11*

How productive (or otherwise!)
has today been for you?

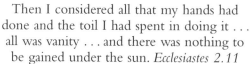

20 _____ •_____

_____

_____

20 _____ •_____

_____

_____

20 _____ •_____

_____

_____

20 _____ •_____

_____

_____

20 _____ •_____

_____

_____

23

July

God arranged the members in the body, each one of them, as he chose . . . There are many members, yet one body.
1 Corinthians 12.18, 20

What are you involved in at your church?

20 _____ •_____

_____

_____

20 _____ •_____

_____

_____

20 _____ •_____

_____

_____

20 _____ •_____

_____

_____

20 _____ •_____

_____

_____

Give your servant therefore an understanding mind to govern your people, able to discern between good and evil; for who can govern this your great people? *1 Kings 3.9*

Which (current or past) world leader do you admire? Why?

20 ___ •_____

_____

_____

20 ___ •_____

_____

_____

20 ___ •_____

_____

_____

20 ___ •_____

_____

_____

20 ___ •_____

_____

_____

25

July

Then Jesus said to them, 'I ask you, is it lawful to do good or to do harm on the sabbath, to save life or to destroy it?'
Luke 6.9

Do you have the opportunity to treat Sundays differently from other days of the week?

20 _____ •

20 _____ •

20 _____ •

20 _____ •

20 _____ •

July

26

Indeed, this is our boast ... we have behaved in the world with frankness and godly sincerity, not by earthly wisdom but by the grace of God. *2 Corinthians 1.12*

Who, for you, exhibits godly sincerity and grace?

20 _____ •_____

_____

_____

20 _____ •_____

_____

_____

20 _____ •_____

_____

_____

20 _____ •_____

_____

_____

20 _____ •_____

_____

_____

_____

27

July

For you, O LORD, have made me glad by your
work; at the works of your hands I sing for joy.
Psalm 92.4

When did you last 'sing for joy'?

20 _____

20 _____

20 _____

20 _____

20 _____

July

28

The Rock, his work is perfect, and
all his ways are just. A faithful God,
without deceit, just and upright is he.
Deuteronomy 32.4

What has God done for you this year
that you'll always remember?

20 _____ •_____

_____

_____

_____

20 _____ •_____

_____

_____

_____

20 _____ •_____

_____

_____

_____

20 _____ •_____

_____

_____

_____

20 _____ •_____

_____

_____

_____

29

July

Do not worry about anything, but in everything by prayer and supplication with thanksgiving let your requests be made known to God. *Philippians 4.6*

What could you stop worrying about (right now!)?

20 ____ •_____

_____

_____

20 ____ •_____

_____

_____

20 ____ •_____

_____

_____

20 ____ •_____

_____

_____

20 ____ •_____

_____

_____

July

30

He removed the high places, broke down
the pillars, and cut down the sacred pole.
He broke in pieces the bronze serpent
that Moses had made. *2 Kings 18.4*

In what way might God be calling you
to set an example to others?

20 ____ •

20 ____ •

20 ____ •

20 ____ •

20 ____ •

31

July

He took him aside in private, away from
the crowd, and put his fingers into his ears,
and he spat and touched his tongue.
Mark 7.33

Whose life have you touched for the better?

20 _____ •_____

_____

_____

20 _____ •_____

_____

_____

20 _____ •_____

_____

_____

20 _____ •_____

_____

_____

20 _____ •_____

_____

_____

_____

August

I appeal to you therefore . . . to present your
bodies as a living sacrifice, holy and acceptable
to God, which is your spiritual worship.
Romans 12.1

Do you feel it's getting easier to
believe God loves you as you are?

20 _____ •_____

_____

_____

_____

20 _____ •_____

_____

_____

_____

20 _____ •_____

_____

_____

_____

20 _____ •_____

_____

_____

_____

20 _____ •_____

_____

_____

_____

August

I will give thanks to the LORD with my whole
heart; I will tell of all your wonderful deeds.
Psalm 9.1

When did you last feel God prompting
you to tell someone about your faith?

20 _____ •

20 _____ •

20 _____ •

20 _____ •

20 _____ •

August

Set your minds on things that are above,
not on things that are on earth.
Colossians 3.2

What brings you pleasure?
How might this glorify God?

20 _____ •_____

_____

_____

20 _____ •_____

_____

_____

20 _____ •_____

_____

_____

20 _____ •_____

_____

_____

20 _____ •_____

_____

_____

_____

4

August

They should make them days of feasting and gladness, days for sending gifts of food to one another and presents to the poor.
Esther 9.22

Who are you supporting financially or emotionally?

20 _____ •_____

_____

_____

20 _____ •_____

_____

_____

20 _____ •_____

_____

_____

20 _____ •_____

_____

_____

20 _____ •_____

_____

_____

August

5

Jesus said to him, 'Stand up, take
your mat and walk.'
John 5.8

When you last prayed for healing,
how was your prayer answered?

20 _____ •_____

_____

_____

20 _____ •_____

_____

_____

20 _____ •_____

_____

_____

20 _____ •_____

_____

_____

20 _____ •_____

_____

_____

_____

6

August

But I did not [lord it over the people],
because of the fear of God.
Nehemiah 5.15

How does your devotion to God
affect your behaviour?

20 ____ •

20 ____ •

20 ____ •

20 ____ •

20 ____ •

August

7

Above all, maintain constant love for one
another, for love covers a multitude of sins.
1 Peter 4.8

Are there people in your life you find
easier to forgive than others?

20 _____ •_____

_____

_____

20 _____ •_____

_____

_____

20 _____ •_____

_____

_____

20 _____ •_____

_____

_____

20 _____ •_____

_____

_____

_____

August

*Keep your heart with all vigilance,
for from it flow the springs of life.*
Proverbs 4.23

What are the books, films, paintings, etc. that
have had an impact on you recently?

20 _____ •_____

20 _____ •_____

20 _____ •_____

20 _____ •_____

20 _____ •_____

August

Six days later, Jesus took with him Peter and
James and his brother John and led them
up a high mountain, by themselves.
Matthew 17.1

Whose company do you find inspiring?

20 _____ •_____

_____

_____

20 _____ •_____

_____

_____

20 _____ •_____

_____

_____

20 _____ •_____

_____

_____

20 _____ •_____

_____

_____

10

August

But exhort one another every day, as long as
it is called 'today', so that none of you may
be hardened by the deceitfulness of sin.
Hebrews 3.13

Did you encourage someone today
and, if so, how?

20 _____ •

20 _____ •

20 _____ •

20 _____ •

20 _____ •

August

11

This is the day that the LORD has made;
let us rejoice and be glad in it.
Psalm 118.24

Which day of the week do you most
enjoy (honestly!)?

20 _____ • _____

_____

_____

20 _____ • _____

_____

_____

20 _____ • _____

_____

_____

20 _____ • _____

_____

_____

20 _____ • _____

_____

_____

12

August

There is therefore now no condemnation for those who are in Christ Jesus. For the law of the Spirit of life in Christ Jesus has set you free.
Romans 8.1–2

Is there a failure in your life that you find it hard to feel is forgiven?

20 ____•

20 ____•

20 ____•

20 ____•

20 ____•

August

13

The LORD stirred up the spirit of
King Cyrus of Persia so that he sent
a herald throughout all his kingdom.
Ezra 1.1

How do you see God working in
the world just now?

20 _____ •_____

_____

_____

_____

20 _____ •_____

_____

_____

_____

20 _____ •_____

_____

_____

_____

20 _____ •_____

_____

_____

_____

20 _____ •_____

_____

_____

_____

14

August

God . . . will not let you be tested beyond your strength, but with the testing he will also provide the way out so that you may be able to endure it. *1 Corinthians 10.13*

Is there a recent time when you have felt tested beyond your strength?

20 _____ •_____

_____

_____

20 _____ •_____

_____

_____

20 _____ •_____

_____

_____

20 _____ •_____

_____

_____

20 _____ •_____

_____

_____

August   **15**

'For God so loved the world, that he gave his
only Son, so that everyone who believes in him
may not perish but may have eternal life.'
John 3.16

Who do you know who has recently
come to faith?

20 _____ •_____
_____
_____

20 _____ •_____
_____
_____

20 _____ •_____
_____
_____

20 _____ •_____
_____
_____

20 _____ •_____
_____
_____
_____

16

August

The LORD said to Abraham, 'Why did Sarah laugh, and say, "Shall I indeed bear a child, now that I am old?" Is anything too wonderful for the LORD?' *Genesis 18.13–14*

Have you ever thought that something was too difficult for God?

20 ___ •_____

_____

_____

_____

20 ___ •_____

_____

_____

_____

20 ___ •_____

_____

_____

_____

20 ___ •_____

_____

_____

_____

20 ___ •_____

_____

_____

_____

August

17

Do not be conformed to this world, but be transformed by the renewing of your minds, so that you may discern what is the will of God.
Romans 12.2

What could you do this week to delight God?

20 _____ •_____

_____

_____

20 _____ •_____

_____

_____

20 _____ •_____

_____

_____

20 _____ •_____

_____

_____

20 _____ •_____

_____

_____

18

August

Hear my prayer, O LORD; give ear
to my supplications in your faithfulness;
answer me in your righteousness.
Psalm 143

In what ways did you need help
from God today?

20 _____ •

20 _____ •

20 _____ •

20 _____ •

20 _____ •

August

19

'What no eye has seen, nor ear heard, nor the human heart conceived, what God has prepared for those who love him' – these things God has revealed to us through the Spirit.
1 Corinthians 2.9–10

What (earthly delights!) are you looking forward to right now?

20 _____

20 _____

20 _____

20 _____

20 _____

20

August

[God] does not retain his anger for ever,
because he delights in showing clemency.
Micah 7.18

How did you cope when you last felt angry?

20 _____ •

20 _____ •

20 _____ •

20 _____ •

20 _____ •

August

Do not judge, and you will not be judged; do not
condemn, and you will not be condemned.
Luke 6.37

What tends to bring out judgemental
feelings in you and why might this be?

20 _____ •

20 _____ •

20 _____ •

20 _____ •

20 _____ •

22

August

There is no fear in love, but perfect love casts out fear; for fear has to do with punishment, and whoever fears has not reached perfection in love. *1 John 4.18*

Is there a person (or a pet) who loves you unconditionally?

20 ____ • _____

_____

_____

20 ____ • _____

_____

_____

20 ____ • _____

_____

_____

20 ____ • _____

_____

_____

20 ____ • _____

_____

_____

August

23

The winter is past, the rain is over and gone.
The flowers appear on the earth;
the time of singing has come.
Song of Solomon 2.11–12

When did you last enjoy a day in the
countryside or at the seaside?

20 _____ •_____

20 _____ •_____

20 _____ •_____

20 _____ •_____

20 _____ •_____

24

August

Greet Mary, who has worked very hard among you. Greet Andronicus and Junia . . . who . . . were in Christ before I was.
Romans 16.6–7

Is there someone whose personality or gifts you particularly admire?

20 _____ •_____

_____

_____

20 _____ •_____

_____

_____

20 _____ •_____

_____

_____

20 _____ •_____

_____

_____

20 _____ •_____

_____

_____

August

One thing I asked of the LORD . . . to live in
the house of the LORD all the days of my life,
to behold the beauty of the LORD, and to
inquire in his temple. *Psalm 27.4*

When or where did you spend time
with God today?

20 _____ •_____

_____

_____

20 _____ •_____

_____

_____

20 _____ •_____

_____

_____

20 _____ •_____

_____

_____

20 _____ •_____

_____

_____

26

August

'Whenever you stand praying, forgive, if
you have anything against anyone; so that
your Father in heaven may also forgive
you your trespasses.' *Mark 11.25*

Who are you struggling to forgive?

20 _____•

20 _____•

20 _____•

20 _____•

20 _____•

August

27

But you will receive power when the
Holy Spirit has come upon you; and you will
be my witnesses in Jerusalem . . . and
to the ends of the earth. *Acts 1.8*

Can you think of a recent event or situation
in which the Holy Spirit was clearly at work?

20 ____ •_____

_____

_____

20 ____ •_____

_____

_____

20 ____ •_____

_____

_____

20 ____ •_____

_____

_____

20 ____ •_____

_____

_____

_____

28

August

We are afflicted in every way, but not crushed; perplexed, but not driven to despair; persecuted, but not forsaken; struck down, but not destroyed. *2 Corinthians 4.8–9*

Did this passage seem especially relevant today – or some time recently?

20 _____ •

_____

_____

_____

20 _____ •

_____

_____

_____

20 _____ •

_____

_____

_____

20 _____ •

_____

_____

_____

20 _____ •

_____

_____

_____

August

29

The people . . . made Saul king before
the LORD in Gilgal. There they sacrificed
offerings of well-being before the
LORD, and . . . rejoiced greatly.
1 Samuel 11.15

How do you celebrate great events?

20 _____ •_____

_____

_____

20 _____ •_____

_____

_____

20 _____ •_____

_____

_____

20 _____ •_____

_____

_____

20 _____ •_____

_____

_____

_____

30

August

And my God will fully satisfy every need of yours according to his riches in glory in Christ Jesus. *Philippians 4.19*

What personal need would you most like God to meet?

20 _____ •_____

_____

_____

20 _____ •_____

_____

_____

20 _____ •_____

_____

_____

20 _____ •_____

_____

_____

20 _____ •_____

_____

_____

August

31

The LORD is slow to anger but great in power,
and the LORD will by no means clear the guilty.
His way is in whirlwind and storm.
Nahum 1.3

Which situation in the world most worries
you? How reassuring is this passage?

20 _____ •

20 _____ •

20 _____ •

20 _____ •

20 _____ •

September

'Ask, and it will be given to you . . .
For everyone who asks receives, and everyone
who searches finds, and for everyone who
knocks, the door will be opened.'
Luke 11.9–10

Have you struggled with doubt today?

20 _____ •

20 _____ •

20 _____ •

20 _____ •

20 _____ •

September

2

We always give thanks to God for all of you
and mention you in our prayers, constantly.
1 Thessalonians 1.2

How do you feel when someone offers
assurance that they're praying for you?

20 ___ •_____

_____

_____

20 ___ •_____

_____

_____

20 ___ •_____

_____

_____

20 ___ •_____

_____

_____

20 ___ •_____

_____

_____

3

September

Surely goodness and mercy shall follow me all
the days of my life, and I shall dwell in the
house of the LORD my whole life long.
Psalm 23.6

Can you think of a moment today when you
were aware of God's goodness?

20 _____ •

20 _____ •

20 _____ •

20 _____ •

20 _____ •

September

4

'And forgive us our debts, as we
also have forgiven our debtors.'
Matthew 6.12

Are you holding any grudges?
If so, what about?

20 _____ •_____

_____

_____

_____

20 _____ •_____

_____

_____

_____

20 _____ •_____

_____

_____

_____

20 _____ •_____

_____

_____

_____

20 _____ •_____

_____

_____

_____

5

September

'For [Aaron] shall not enter the land that I have
given to the Israelites, because you rebelled against
my command at the waters of Meribah.'
Numbers 20.24

Do you know someone who is struggling
in their relationship with God?

20 _____

_____

_____

20 _____

_____

_____

20 _____

_____

_____

20 _____

_____

_____

20 _____

_____

_____

_____

September

6

I have heard of your faith in the Lord Jesus
and your love towards all the saints.
Ephesians 1.15

Did you get an opportunity to show
God's love to someone today?

20 _____ • _____

20 _____ • _____

20 _____ • _____

20 _____ • _____

20 _____ • _____

7 September

'In my Father's house there are many dwelling-
places. If it were not so, would I have told you
that I go to prepare a place for you?'
John 14.2

Have you spent time contemplating
your own death?

20 _____ •

20 _____ •

20 _____ •

20 _____ •

20 _____ •

September

'We have sinned and done wrong, acted wickedly and rebelled, turning aside from your commandments and ordinances.'
Daniel 9.5

What do you need to confess to God today?

20 _____ •_____

_____

_____

20 _____ •_____

_____

_____

_____

20 _____ •_____

_____

_____

_____

20 _____ •_____

_____

_____

_____

20 _____ •_____

_____

_____

_____

September

For he will repay according to each one's deeds.
Romans 2.6

Is there someone you misjudged at
first but have come to appreciate?

20 _____ •

20 _____ •

20 _____ •

20 _____ •

20 _____ •

September

10

For which of you, intending to build a tower,
does not first sit down and estimate the cost, to
see whether he has enough to complete it?
Luke 14.28

What are you saving towards at the moment?

20 _____ •_____

_____

_____

20 _____ •_____

_____

_____

20 _____ •_____

_____

_____

20 _____ •_____

_____

_____

20 _____ •_____

_____

_____

11

September

I will praise the LORD as long as I live; I will
sing praises to my God all my life long.
Psalm 146.2

How do you most enjoy praising God?

20 ___ •_____

20 ___ •_____

20 ___ •_____

20 ___ •_____

20 ___ •_____

September 12

Do not neglect to do good and to share what you have, for such sacrifices are pleasing to God.
Hebrews 13.16

What did you last do that felt sacrificial?

20 ___ •_____

_____

_____

20 ___ •_____

_____

_____

20 ___ •_____

_____

_____

20 ___ •_____

_____

_____

20 ___ •_____

_____

_____

_____

 **13**

September

And we sent Timothy, our brother and
co-worker for God in proclaiming the gospel of
Christ, to strengthen and encourage you for
the sake of your faith. *1 Thessalonians 3.2*

Who has 'strengthened and encouraged
you' in your faith recently?

20 _____

20 _____

20 _____

20 _____

20 _____

September 14

In all your ways acknowledge him, and he
will make straight your paths.
Proverbs 3.6

In what aspect of your daily life do you
feel God is helping you most?

20 _____ •_____

_____

_____

20 _____ •_____

_____

_____

20 _____ •_____

_____

_____

20 _____ •_____

_____

_____

20 _____ •_____

_____

_____

15

September

And the tongue is a fire. The tongue is
placed among our members as a world of
iniquity; it stains the whole body.
James 3.6

How do you act after you've said
something you deeply regret?

20 _____ •_____

_____

_____

20 _____ •_____

_____

_____

20 _____ •_____

_____

_____

20 _____ •_____

_____

_____

20 _____ •_____

_____

_____

September

16

He ordered them to take nothing for
their journey except a staff; no bread,
no bag, no money in their belts.
Mark 6.8

Are there any things you feel you
would struggle to live without?

20 _____ •_____

_____

_____

20 _____ •_____

_____

_____

20 _____ •_____

_____

_____

20 _____ •_____

_____

_____

20 _____ •_____

_____

_____

_____

 **September**

Above all, clothe yourselves with love, which
binds everything together in perfect harmony.
Colossians 3.14

Is there anyone you are finding it
difficult to love at the moment?

20 _____ •_____

_____

_____

20 _____ •_____

_____

_____

20 _____ •_____

_____

_____

20 _____ •_____

_____

_____

20 _____ •_____

_____

_____

September

18

As a deer longs for flowing streams,
so my soul longs for you, O God.
Psalm 42.1

Where do you feel closest to God?

20 ___ •

20 ___ •

20 ___ •

20 ___ •

20 ___ •

19

September

We know that all things work together
for good for those who love God, who
are called according to his purpose.
Romans 8.28

Can you think of a problem that has been
overcome in a way you didn't expect?

20 _____ •_____

_____

_____

20 _____ •_____

_____

_____

20 _____ •_____

_____

_____

20 _____ •_____

_____

_____

20 _____ •_____

_____

_____

September

20

'Go your way, eat the fat and drink sweet wine
and send portions of them to those for whom
nothing is prepared, for this day is holy to
our LORD.' *Nehemiah 8.10*

In what ways is your church
helping those in need?

20 _____ •_____

_____

_____

_____

20 _____ •_____

_____

_____

_____

20 _____ •_____

_____

_____

_____

20 _____ •_____

_____

_____

_____

20 _____ •_____

_____

_____

_____

# 21

September

'I am the vine, you are the branches. Those who abide in me and I in them bear much fruit, because apart from me you can do nothing.'
John 15.5

What would the perfect you be like?

20 _____ •

20 _____ •

20 _____ •

20 _____ •

20 _____ •

September

22

God is our refuge and strength, a very present
help in trouble. Therefore we will not fear,
though the earth should change, though
the mountains shake. *Psalm 46. 1–2*

What current situation in the world
are you fervently trusting to God?

20 _____ •_____

_____

_____

20 _____ •_____

_____

_____

20 _____ •_____

_____

_____

20 _____ •_____

_____

_____

20 _____ •_____

_____

_____

_____

23

September

As God's chosen ones, holy and beloved,
clothe yourselves with compassion,
kindness, humility, meekness, and patience.
Colossians 3.12

When did you last perform a
random act of kindness?

20 ____ •_____

_____

_____

20 ____ •_____

_____

_____

_____

20 ____ •_____

_____

_____

_____

20 ____ •_____

_____

_____

_____

20 ____ •_____

_____

_____

_____

_____

September

24

They devoted themselves to the apostles'
teaching and fellowship, to the breaking
of bread and the prayers.
Acts 2.42

What was the subject of the
last sermon you heard?

20 _____ •_____

_____

_____

20 _____ •_____

_____

_____

20 _____ •_____

_____

_____

20 _____ •_____

_____

_____

20 _____ •_____

_____

_____

_____

25

September

I will rejoice in Jerusalem, and delight in my
people; no more shall the sound of weeping
be heard in it, or the cry of distress.
Isaiah 65.19

Is there someone you know who is grieving?

20 _____ •

20 _____ •

20 _____ •

20 _____ •

20 _____ •

September

26

Whatever is true, whatever is honourable, whatever is just, whatever is pure . . . if there is anything worthy of praise, think about these things. *Philippians 4.8*

What are you doing to nourish your inner life?

20 _____ • _____

_____

_____

20 _____ • _____

_____

_____

20 _____ • _____

_____

_____

20 _____ • _____

_____

_____

20 _____ • _____

_____

_____

_____

27 September

'But as for [the seed] in the good soil, these
are the ones who, when they hear the word,
hold it fast in an honest and good heart.'
Luke 8.15

Which of your qualities do you think
God most delights in?

20 _____

20 _____

20 _____

20 _____

20 _____

September

But the serpent said to the woman, 'You will not die; for God knows that when you eat of it your eyes will be opened, and you will be like God . . .' *Genesis 3.4–5*

When was the last time you did something you came to regret?

20 _____ •_____

_____

_____

20 _____ •_____

_____

_____

_____

20 _____ •_____

_____

_____

_____

20 _____ •_____

_____

_____

_____

20 _____ •_____

_____

_____

_____

29

September

Cast your burden on the LORD,
and he will sustain you; he will never
permit the righteous to be moved.
Psalm 55.22

What are you struggling with at the moment?

20 _____ •_____

20 _____ •_____

20 _____ •_____

20 _____ •_____

20 _____ •_____

September

30

I thank my God every time I remember
you, constantly praying with joy in every
one of my prayers for all of you.
Philippians 1.3–4

Who or what brought joy into your life today?

20 _____ •_____

20 _____ •_____

20 _____ •_____

20 _____ •_____

20 _____ •_____

October

Where then is my hope?
Who will see my hope?
Job 17.15

What sustains you from day to day?

20 _____ •_____

_____

_____

20 _____ •_____

_____

_____

20 _____ •_____

_____

_____

20 _____ •_____

_____

_____

20 _____ •_____

_____

_____

October

'As the Father has loved me, so I have
loved you; abide in my love.'
John 15.9

What does it mean to you to
'abide' in Christ's love?

20 ___ •

20 ___ •

20 ___ •

20 ___ •

20 ___ •

3

October

May the Lord direct your hearts to the love of
God and to the steadfastness of Christ.
2 Thessalonians 3.5

Why did you last feel impatient with God?

20 ___ • _____

_____

_____

20 ___ • _____

_____

_____

20 ___ • _____

_____

_____

20 ___ • _____

_____

_____

20 ___ • _____

_____

_____

_____

October

4

For if they fall, one will lift up the other;
but woe to one who is alone and falls
and does not have another to help.
Ecclesiastes 4.10

Who are the people who most appreciate
your love and support?

20 _____ •_____

_____

_____

20 _____ •_____

_____

_____

20 _____ •_____

_____

_____

20 _____ •_____

_____

_____

20 _____ •_____

_____

_____

5

October

'Give us this day our daily bread.'
Matthew 6.11

How has God provided for your needs today?

20 _____ •

20 _____ •

20 _____ •

20 _____ •

20 _____ •

October

6

Bear with one another and, if anyone has a complaint against another, forgive each other; just as the Lord has forgiven you, so you also must forgive. *Colossians 3.13*

Has someone deliberately hurt you recently? If so, how did you respond?

20 ___ •_____

_____

_____

20 ___ •_____

_____

_____

20 ___ •_____

_____

_____

20 ___ •_____

_____

_____

20 ___ •_____

_____

_____

October

He said, 'My presence will go with you,
and I will give you rest.'
Exodus 33.14

When did you enjoy 'rest' today?

20 _____ •

20 _____ •

20 _____ •

20 _____ •

20 _____ •

October

Praise the LORD! How good it is to sing
praises to our God; for he is gracious,
and a song of praise is fitting.
Psalm 147.1

What is your favourite hymn or
song at the moment?

20 _____ •_____

_____

_____

20 _____ •_____

_____

_____

20 _____ •_____

_____

_____

20 _____ •_____

_____

_____

20 _____ •_____

_____

_____

October

Blessed is anyone who endures temptation.
Such a one has stood the test and will receive
the crown of life that the Lord has promised
to those who love him. *James 1.12*

Who do you know who is going
through a testing time?

20 _____ •

20 _____ •

20 _____ •

20 _____ •

20 _____ •

October

'Peace I leave with you; my peace I give to
you. I do not give to you as the world gives.
Do not let your hearts be troubled, and do
not let them be afraid.' *John 14.27*

Reflect on this verse for a few moments.
How does it make you feel?

20 _____ •_____

_____

_____

20 _____ •_____

_____

_____

20 _____ •_____

_____

_____

20 _____ •_____

_____

_____

20 _____ •_____

_____

_____

_____

11

October

O LORD, how long shall I cry for help,
and you will not listen? Or cry to you
'Violence!' and you will not save?
Habakkuk 1.2

How do you cope when God seems silent?

20 _____ •

20 _____ •

20 _____ •

20 _____ •

20 _____ •

October

12

Now may our Lord Jesus Christ himself and
God our Father, who loved us . . . comfort
your hearts and strengthen them in every good
work and word. *2 Thessalonians 2.16–17*

What one thing would you most like
to do for God?

20 _____ •_____

_____

_____

20 _____ •_____

_____

_____

20 _____ •_____

_____

_____

20 _____ •_____

_____

_____

20 _____ •_____

_____

_____

13

October

But Jonah set out to flee to Tarshish
from the presence of the LORD.
Jonah 1.3

Have you felt yourself turning away
from God recently? Why?

20 _____

20 _____

20 _____

20 _____

20 _____

October

14

'This is my commandment, that you love
one another as I have loved you.'
John 15.12

What practical action might be involved
in loving people as Jesus loves you?

20 _____ •_____

_____

_____

20 _____ •_____

_____

_____

20 _____ •_____

_____

_____

20 _____ •_____

_____

_____

20 _____ •_____

_____

_____

15

October

From the rising of the sun to its setting
the name of the LORD is to be praised.
Psalm 113.3

How did you feel when you
got up this morning?

20 _____ •_____

20 _____ •_____

20 _____ •_____

20 _____ •_____

20 _____ •_____

October

16

May the grace of our Lord Jesus Christ be
with your spirit, brothers and sisters. Amen.
Galatians 6.18

If St Paul were to write to your church,
what would his main message be?

20 _____ •_____

_____

_____

20 _____ •_____

_____

_____

20 _____ •_____

_____

_____

20 _____ •_____

_____

_____

20 _____ •_____

_____

_____

_____

17 October

'Therefore I tell you, do not worry ... what you will eat or what you will drink ... And can any of you by worrying add a single hour to your span of life?' *Matthew 6.25, 27*

What might you do with all the time you currently spend worrying (uselessly!)?

20 _____ •_____

_____

_____

20 _____ •_____

_____

_____

20 _____ •_____

_____

_____

20 _____ •_____

_____

_____

20 _____ •_____

_____

_____

October

'O that I might have my request,
and that God would grant my desire.'
Job 6.8

What prayer of yours has God
answered recently?

20 _____ •_____

_____

_____

20 _____ •_____

_____

_____

20 _____ •_____

_____

_____

20 _____ •_____

_____

_____

20 _____ •_____

_____

_____

19

October

Put to death, therefore, whatever in you is
earthly: fornication, impurity, passion, evil
desire, and greed (which is idolatry).
Colossians 3.5

Looking back over the past few months, what
has contributed to your spiritual growth?

20 _____ •_____

20 _____ •_____

20 _____ •_____

20 _____ •_____

20 _____ •_____

October

20

So we can say with confidence,
'The Lord is my helper; I will not be afraid.
What can anyone do to me?'
Hebrews 13.6

Who intimidates you? Does this verse
help you in any way?

20 _____ •_____

_____

_____

20 _____ •_____

_____

_____

20 _____ •_____

_____

_____

20 _____ •_____

_____

_____

20 _____ •_____

_____

_____

 **21** October

The spirit of the Lord GOD is upon me, because the LORD has anointed me; he has sent me to bring good news to the oppressed.
Isaiah 61.1

What stops you from sharing the good news of Jesus with others?

20 _____ •_____

20 _____ •_____

20 _____ •_____

20 _____ •_____

20 _____ •_____

October

22

'Your kingdom come. Your will be done,
on earth as it is in heaven.'
Matthew 6.10

How are you seeking to express the way of
Christ rather than the way of the world?

20 ____ •

20 ____ •

20 ____ •

20 ____ •

20 ____ •

October

Take the helmet of salvation, and the sword
of the Spirit, which is the word of God.
Ephesians 6.17

Have you been conscious of coming
under spiritual attack?

20 _____ •_____

_____

_____

20 _____ •_____

_____

_____

20 _____ •_____

_____

_____

20 _____ •_____

_____

_____

20 _____ •_____

_____

_____

October

24

The LORD is near to all who call on him, to all who call on him in truth . . . The LORD watches over all who love him.
Psalm 145.18, 20

Have you felt God's nearness to you today?

20 _____ •_____

_____

_____

20 _____ •_____

_____

_____

20 _____ •_____

_____

_____

20 _____ •_____

_____

20 _____ •_____

_____

_____

_____

25

October

Then the devil took him to Jerusalem, and placed him on the pinnacle of the temple ... Jesus answered him, 'It is said, "Do not put the Lord your God to the test."' *Luke 4.9, 12*

What strategies do you have for coping with temptation?

20 _____ •_____

_____

_____

20 _____ •_____

_____

_____

20 _____ •_____

_____

_____

20 _____ •_____

_____

_____

20 _____ •_____

_____

_____

October

26

A new heart I will give you, and a new spirit
I will put within you; and I will remove from
your body the heart of stone and give
you a heart of flesh. *Ezekiel 36.26*

Have you felt your spirits lifted by
some event today?

20 _____ •_____

_____

_____

20 _____ •_____

_____

_____

20 _____ •_____

_____

_____

20 _____ •_____

_____

_____

20 _____ •_____

_____

_____

_____

27

October

But if we walk in the light as he himself is in the light, we have fellowship with one another, and the blood of Jesus his Son cleanses us from all sin.
1 John 1.7

What does 'fellowship' mean to you?

20 _____ .

20 _____ .

20 _____ .

20 _____ .

20 _____ .

October

For I am about to create new heavens and
a new earth; the former things shall not
be remembered or come to mind.
Isaiah 65.17

What aspect of God's creation have
you enjoyed this week?

20 _____ •_____

_____

_____

20 _____ •_____

_____

_____

20 _____ •_____

_____

_____

20 _____ •_____

_____

_____

20 _____ •_____

_____

_____

_____

29

October

'Do to others as you would have them do to you.' *Luke 6.31*

What would you love someone to do for you this week?

20 _____

20 _____

20 _____

20 _____

20 _____

October

They went into the ark with Noah, two and two of all flesh in which there was the breath of life. *Genesis 7.15*

What is your favourite animal? Why?

20 _____ •

20 _____ •

20 _____ •

20 _____ •

20 _____ •

31

October

Do not lag in zeal,
be ardent in spirit, serve the Lord.
Romans 12.11

When did you last experience a time of
consolation or a time of desolation?

20 _____ . _____

_____

_____

20 _____ . _____

_____

_____

20 _____ . _____

_____

_____

20 _____ . _____

_____

_____

20 _____ . _____

_____

_____

November

1

He called the twelve and began to
send them out two by two, and gave them
authority over the unclean spirits.
Mark 6.7

Has it been easier to tell people about your faith
when another Christian has been with you?

20 _____ •_____

_____

_____

20 _____ •_____

_____

_____

20 _____ •_____

_____

_____

20 _____ •_____

_____

_____

20 _____ •_____

_____

_____

November

*From Mount Hor they set out by the way to the
Red Sea, to go around the land of Edom; but
the people became impatient on the way.*
Numbers 21.4

How at peace or restless do you
feel at the moment?

20 _____ •_____
_____
_____

20 _____ •_____
_____
_____

20 _____ •_____
_____
_____

20 _____ •_____
_____
_____

20 _____ •_____
_____
_____

November

3

Let the heavens be glad, and let the earth
rejoice; let the sea roar . . . Then shall all
the trees of the forest sing for joy.
Psalm 96.11–12

Where is your favourite place in the world?

20 _____ •_____

_____

_____

20 _____ •_____

_____

_____

20 _____ •_____

_____

_____

20 _____ •_____

_____

_____

20 _____ •_____

_____

_____

_____

4

November

Blessed be the God and Father of our
Lord Jesus Christ, the Father of mercies
and the God of all consolation.
2 Corinthians 1.3

When did you find comfort
in God's love today?

20 _____ • _____

_____

_____

20 _____ • _____

_____

_____

20 _____ • _____

_____

_____

20 _____ • _____

_____

_____

20 _____ • _____

_____

_____

November

5

'But when this son of yours came back, who
has devoured your property with prostitutes,
you killed the fatted calf for him!'
Luke 15.30

How do you cope with unfairness –
perceived or actual?

20 _____ •_____

_____

_____

20 _____ •_____

_____

_____

20 _____ •_____

_____

_____

20 _____ •_____

_____

_____

20 _____ •_____

_____

_____

_____

6 November

'Suppose five of the fifty righteous are lacking?
Will you destroy the whole city for lack of five?'
And he said, 'I will not destroy it if I find
forty-five there.' *Genesis 18.28*

Can you think of a time when you
bargained with God?

20 _____ •

20 _____ •

20 _____ •

20 _____ •

20 _____ •

November

7

Pray in the Spirit at all times in every prayer and supplication. To that end keep alert and always persevere in supplication for all the saints.
Ephesians 6.18

How often did you turn to God
in prayer today?

20 ____ • _____

_____

_____

20 ____ • _____

_____

_____

20 ____ • _____

_____

_____

20 ____ • _____

_____

_____

20 ____ • _____

_____

_____

November

8

You shall not wrong or oppress a resident alien,
for you were aliens in the land of Egypt.
Exodus 22.21

How many different cultures or nationalities
are represented in your church?

20 _____ •_____

_____

_____

20 _____ •_____

_____

_____

20 _____ •_____

_____

_____

20 _____ •_____

_____

_____

20 _____ •_____

_____

_____

_____

November

9

And he said to them, 'Take care! Be on your guard
against all kinds of greed; for one's life does not
consist in the abundance of possessions.'
Luke 12.15

What do you own that you find hard
to share with others?

20 ____ •_____

_____

_____

20 ____ •_____

_____

_____

20 ____ •_____

_____

_____

20 ____ •_____

_____

_____

20 ____ •_____

_____

_____

10

November

Praise the LORD, all you nations! Extol him,
all you peoples! For great is his steadfast love
towards us, and the faithfulness of the LORD
endures for ever. Praise the LORD!
Psalm 117

Who has been your most faithful friend?

20 _____ •

20 _____ •

20 _____ •

20 _____ •

20 _____ •

November

11

So we do not lose heart. Even though our
outer nature is wasting away, our inner
nature is being renewed day by day.
2 Corinthians 4.16

What are your concerns about getting older?

20 ____ •_____

_____

_____

20 ____ •_____

_____

_____

20 ____ •_____

_____

_____

20 ____ •_____

_____

_____

20 ____ •_____

_____

_____

12 November

My God, my rock, in whom I take refuge,
my shield and the horn of my salvation,
my stronghold and my refuge, my saviour;
you save me from violence. *2 Samuel 22.3*

What is one thing you might do this
week to promote the way of peace?

20 _____ • _____

_____

_____

20 _____ • _____

_____

_____

20 _____ • _____

_____

_____

20 _____ • _____

_____

_____

20 _____ • _____

_____

_____

November

13

But in your hearts sanctify Christ as Lord. Always be ready to make your defence to anyone who demands from you an accounting of the hope that is in you. *1 Peter 3.15*

When you've shared your personal testimony with someone, how has he/she responded?

20 ____ •_____

_____

_____

20 ____ •_____

_____

_____

20 ____ •_____

_____

_____

20 ____ •_____

_____

_____

20 ____ •_____

_____

_____

14

November

The name of the LORD is a strong tower;
the righteous run into it and are safe.
Proverbs 18.10

When you last faced a challenge,
did you feel God near you?

20 ____ •_____

_____

_____

20 ____ •_____

_____

_____

20 ____ •_____

_____

_____

20 ____ •_____

_____

_____

20 ____ •_____

_____

_____

November 15

In those days John the Baptist appeared in the wilderness of Judea, proclaiming, 'Repent, for the kingdom of heaven has come near.'
Matthew 3.1–2

Can you think of any past injustices carried out by your country that make you feel ashamed?

20 _____ •_____

20 _____ •_____

20 _____ •_____

20 _____ •_____

20 _____ •_____

16 November

When she could hide him no longer she got a papyrus basket for him . . . His sister stood at a distance, to see what would happen to him.
Exodus 2.3–4

Have you done something that required all your faith recently?

20 _____ •_____

_____

_____

20 _____ •_____

_____

_____

20 _____ •_____

_____

_____

20 _____ •_____

_____

_____

20 _____ •_____

_____

_____

November

17

The Lord is not slow about his promise, as some think of slowness, but is patient with you, not wanting any to perish, but all to come to repentance. *2 Peter 3.9*

Is there a prayer you've waited many years to be answered?

20 ___ •_____

_____

_____

20 ___ •_____

_____

_____

20 ___ •_____

_____

_____

20 ___ •_____

_____

_____

20 ___ •_____

_____

_____

18

November

Remember the wonderful works he has done,
his miracles, and the judgements he has uttered.
Psalm 105.5

Reflecting on the day, what event or
encounter stands out most?

20 _____ .⟋_____
_____
_____

20 _____ .⟋_____
_____
_____

20 _____ .⟋_____
_____
_____

20 _____ .⟋_____
_____
_____

20 _____ .⟋_____
_____
_____

November

19

I, I am He who blots out your transgressions for my own sake, and I will not remember your sins.
Isaiah 43.25

Is there someone whose sins you find
hard to forget (if not to forgive)?

20 ____ • _____

_____

_____

_____

20 ____ • _____

_____

_____

_____

20 ____ • _____

_____

_____

20 ____ • _____

_____

_____

20 ____ • _____

_____

_____

_____

20 November

Let your speech always be gracious,
seasoned with salt, so that you may know
how you ought to answer everyone.
Colossians 4.6

Whose company heartens and encourages you?

20 ____ •

20 ____ •

20 ____ •

20 ____ •

20 ____ •

November

21

'Do not store up for yourselves treasures on earth, where moth and rust consume ... but store up for yourselves treasures in heaven.'
Matthew 6.19–20

What personal possession would you most regret losing?

20 _____ •_____

_____

_____

20 _____ •_____

_____

_____

20 _____ •_____

_____

_____

20 _____ •_____

_____

_____

20 _____ •_____

_____

_____

22 November

But Moses' hands grew weary . . . Aaron and
Hur held up his hands, one on one side, and
the other on the other side; so his hands were
steady until the sun set. *Exodus 17.12*

Is there something you've given your
all to for the benefit of others?

20 _____ •_____

_____

_____

20 _____ •_____

_____

_____

20 _____ •_____

_____

_____

20 _____ •_____

_____

_____

20 _____ •_____

_____

_____

November

23

Endurance produces character,
and character produces hope.
Romans 5.4

What character trait do you value most
highly in your friends?

20 _____ •_____

_____

_____

20 _____ •_____

_____

_____

20 _____ •_____

_____

_____

20 _____ •_____

_____

_____

20 _____ •_____

_____

_____

24 November

And the LORD was sorry that he
had made humankind on the earth,
and it grieved him to his heart.
Genesis 6.6

What has been your greatest sadness
this past year?

20 _____•_____

_____

_____

20 _____•_____

_____

_____

20 _____•_____

_____

_____

20 _____•_____

_____

_____

20 _____•_____

_____

_____

November

25

It is these worldly people, devoid of the
Spirit, who are causing divisions.
Jude 19

How well does your church cope with conflict?

20 _____ •_____

20 _____ •_____

20 _____ •_____

20 _____ •_____

20 _____ •_____

26

November

Many are the afflictions of the righteous,
but the LORD rescues them from them all.
Psalm 34.19

Are you waiting for God to rescue you
from anything at the moment?

20 _____ •_____

_____

_____

20 _____ •_____

_____

_____

20 _____ •_____

_____

_____

20 _____ •_____

_____

_____

20 _____ •_____

_____

_____

November

'So do not worry about tomorrow, for
tomorrow will bring worries of its own.
Today's trouble is enough for today.'
Matthew 6.34

Can you remember what you were
worrying about yesterday?

20 _____ •_____

_____

_____

20 _____ •_____

_____

_____

20 _____ •_____

_____

_____

20 _____ •_____

_____

_____

20 _____ •_____

_____

_____

_____

November

Commit your work to the LORD,
and your plans will be established.
Proverbs 16.3

Where do you think God might
lead you over the next year?

20 ____ •

20 ____ •

20 ____ •

20 ____ •

20 ____ •

November

First, I thank my God through Jesus Christ
for all of you, because your faith is
proclaimed throughout the world.
Romans 1.8

Has someone ever said they thanked
God for you? How did that feel?

20 _____ •_____

_____

_____

20 _____ •_____

_____

_____

20 _____ •_____

_____

_____

20 _____ •_____

_____

_____

20 _____ •_____

_____

_____

30

November

Now the word of the LORD came to Jonah . . .
'Go at once to Nineveh . . . and cry out against it;
for their wickedness has come up before me.'
Jonah 1.1–2

Is there a challenge in your life right now that
feels overwhelming?

20 _____

20 _____

20 _____

20 _____

20 _____

December

1

For now we see in a mirror, dimly, but then we will
see face to face. Now I know only in part; then I
will know fully, even as I have been fully known.
1 Corinthians 13.12

How does the fact that God knows and loves
you intimately make you feel about yourself?

20 ___ • _____
_____
_____

20 ___ • _____
_____
_____

20 ___ • _____
_____
_____

20 ___ • _____
_____
_____

20 ___ • _____
_____
_____

December

You are my hiding-place and my shield; I hope in
your word. Go away from me, you evildoers, that
I may keep the commandments of my God.
Psalm 119.114–115

When did you last extricate yourself
from an unhealthy relationship?

20 ___ •_____

_____

_____

20 ___ •_____

_____

_____

20 ___ •_____

_____

_____

20 ___ •_____

_____

_____

20 ___ •_____

_____

_____

December

For I am not ashamed of the gospel; it is the
power of God for salvation to everyone who has
faith, to the Jew first and also to the Greek.
Romans 1.16

Who might you invite to church
over the Christmas period?

20 _____ •_____

_____

_____

20 _____ •_____

_____

_____

20 _____ •_____

_____

_____

20 _____ •_____

_____

_____

20 _____ •_____

_____

_____

_____

December

But some of them said, 'Could not he
who opened the eyes of the blind man
have kept this man from dying?'
John 11.37

Has something happened to you – or someone
you know – that you just can't make sense of?

20 _____ •_____

_____

_____

_____

20 _____ •_____

_____

_____

_____

20 _____ •_____

_____

_____

_____

20 _____ •_____

_____

_____

_____

20 _____ •_____

_____

_____

_____

December

5

Do not envy the wicked, nor
desire to be with them.
Proverbs 24.1

We all fall short in some way – what is
the failing you're most ashamed of?

20 ___ •_____

_____

_____

20 ___ •_____

_____

_____

20 ___ •_____

_____

_____

20 ___ •_____

_____

_____

20 ___ •_____

_____

_____

6

December

Who is wise and understanding among you?
Show by your good life that your works are
done with gentleness born of wisdom.
James 3.13

What would God have found
pleasing about your actions today?

20 _____ •_____

_____

_____

20 _____ •_____

_____

_____

20 _____ •_____

_____

_____

20 _____ •_____

_____

_____

20 _____ •_____

_____

_____

December

7

'For if you forgive others their trespasses,
your heavenly Father will also forgive you.'
Matthew 6.14

How does it feel to be forgiven – by
God or others?

20 _____ •_____

_____

_____

20 _____ •_____

_____

_____

20 _____ •_____

_____

_____

20 _____ •_____

_____

_____

20 _____ •_____

_____

_____

December

I consider that the sufferings of this present time are not worth comparing with the glory about to be revealed to us.
Romans 8.18

Do you feel you are becoming more patient?

20 _____ •_____

_____

_____

20 _____ •_____

_____

_____

20 _____ •_____

_____

_____

20 _____ •_____

_____

_____

20 _____ •_____

_____

_____

December

9

Praise the LORD! Sing to the LORD a new song,
his praise in the assembly of the faithful.
Psalm 149.1

What do you think God loves
about your church?

20 _____ •_____

_____

_____

20 _____ •_____

_____

_____

20 _____ •_____

_____

_____

20 _____ •_____

_____

_____

20 _____ •_____

_____

_____

_____

December

Now may the Lord of peace himself
give you peace at all times in all ways.
The Lord be with all of you.
2 Thessalonians 3.16

How easy has it been to
'let go and let God' today?

20 _____ •_____

_____

_____

20 _____ •_____

_____

_____

20 _____ •_____

_____

_____

20 _____ •_____

_____

_____

20 _____ •_____

_____

_____

December 11

Then the LORD replied with gracious and
comforting words to the angel who talked with me.
Zechariah 1.13

Have you – or has someone you know –
been aware of the presence of angels?

20 _____ •_____

_____

_____

20 _____ •_____

_____

_____

20 _____ •_____

_____

_____

20 _____ •_____

_____

_____

20 _____ •_____

_____

_____

_____

12 December

Our Lord Jesus Christ , . . died for us,
so that whether we are awake or
asleep we may live with him.
1 Thessalonians 5.10

What Bible passages, prayers, hymns or songs
comfort you in the middle of the night?

20 _____ .

20 _____ .

20 _____ .

20 _____ .

20 _____ .

December

13

'Why do you see the speck in your neighbour's eye, but do not notice the log in your own eye?' *Matthew 7.3*

Is there someone you're feeling critical of at the moment?

20 _____ •_____

_____

_____

20 _____ •_____

_____

_____

20 _____ •_____

_____

_____

20 _____ •_____

_____

_____

20 _____ •_____

_____

_____

_____

 **December**

Even though I walk through the darkest valley,
I fear no evil; for you are with me; your rod
and your staff – they comfort me.
Psalm 23.4

How regularly do you encounter spiritual
depression? How do you cope with it?

20 _____ •_____

_____

_____

20 _____ •_____

_____

_____

20 _____ •_____

_____

_____

20 _____ •_____

_____

_____

20 _____ •_____

_____

_____

December

15

Do your best to present yourself to God as one approved by him, a worker who has no need to be ashamed, rightly explaining the word of truth.
2 Timothy 2.15

In what ways do people see your faith at work?

20 _____ •_____

_____

_____

20 _____ •_____

_____

_____

20 _____ •_____

_____

_____

20 _____ •_____

_____

_____

20 _____ •_____

_____

_____

_____

16

December

I am about to do a new thing; now it springs
forth, do you not perceive it? I will make a way
in the wilderness and rivers in the desert.
Isaiah 43.19

Has something happened this past year that
you would never have imagined possible?

20 ___ • _____

_____

_____

20 ___ • _____

_____

_____

20 ___ • _____

_____

_____

20 ___ • _____

_____

_____

20 ___ • _____

_____

_____

December

17

Then he took a cup, and after giving thanks he
said, 'Take this and divide it among yourselves.'
Luke 22.17

When was the last time you celebrated
Holy Communion?

20 _____ •_____

_____

_____

20 _____ •_____

_____

_____

20 _____ •_____

_____

_____

20 _____ •_____

_____

_____

20 _____ •_____

_____

_____

December

This book of the law shall not depart out of your
mouth; you shall meditate on it day and night.
Joshua 1.8

How often do you read the Bible (apart
from when you're using this journal!)?

20 _____ •_____

_____

_____

20 _____ •_____

_____

_____

20 _____ •_____

_____

_____

20 _____ •_____

_____

_____

20 _____ •_____

_____

_____

_____

December

19

Why are you cast down, O my soul, and why are you disquieted within me? Hope in God; for I shall again praise him, my help and my God.
Psalm 42.5

How do you feel about the Christmas season?

20 _____ • _____

20 _____ • _____

20 _____ • _____

20 _____ • _____

20 _____ • _____

20

December

'Ask, and it will be given to you;
search, and you will find; knock, and
the door will be opened for you.'
Matthew 7.7

What would you like to ask
God for this Christmas?

20 _____ •_____

_____

_____

20 _____ •_____

_____

_____

20 _____ •_____

_____

_____

20 _____ •_____

_____

_____

20 _____ •_____

_____

_____

December

21

But the Lord is faithful; he will strengthen
you and guard you from the evil one.
2 Thessalonians 3.3

How could today have been even better?

20 _____ •_____

_____

_____

20 _____ •_____

_____

_____

20 _____ •_____

_____

_____

20 _____ •_____

_____

_____

20 _____ •_____

_____

_____

December

Do not neglect to show hospitality to
strangers, for by doing that some have
entertained angels without knowing it.
Hebrews 13.2

Are you planning to share Christmas
with anyone? If so, who?

20 _____ •_____

_____

_____

20 _____ •_____

_____

_____

20 _____ •_____

_____

_____

20 _____ •_____

_____

_____

20 _____ •_____

_____

_____

December

'But I say to you that listen, Love your enemies, do good to those who hate you, bless those who curse you, pray for those who abuse you.' *Luke 6.27–28*

Are you praying just now for people you find it hard to get on with?

20 ____ •_____

_____

_____

20 ____ •_____

_____

_____

20 ____ •_____

_____

_____

20 ____ •_____

_____

_____

20 ____ •_____

_____

_____

24 December

I know what it is to have little, and I know what it is to have plenty. In any and all circumstances I have learned the secret of being well-fed and of going hungry.
Philippians 4.12–13

Thinking of the world this Christmas Eve, what is your prayer?

20 ____ •_____

_____

_____

20 ____ •_____

_____

_____

20 ____ •_____

_____

_____

20 ____ •_____

_____

_____

20 ____ •_____

_____

_____

December

25

For a child has been born for us, a son given to us . . . and he is named Wonderful Counsellor, Mighty God, Everlasting Father, Prince of Peace. *Isaiah 9.6*

What is your best (or worst!) Christmas Day memory?

20 _____ •_____

_____

_____

20 _____ •_____

_____

_____

20 _____ •_____

_____

_____

20 _____ •_____

_____

_____

20 _____ •_____

_____

_____

 **December**

'Everyone serves the good wine first,
and then the inferior wine after the guests
have become drunk. But you have kept
the good wine until now.' *John 2.10*

What would you like Jesus to change
in you this coming year?

20 ___ •

20 ___ •

20 ___ •

20 ___ •

20 ___ •

December

27

But Moses said to the LORD, 'O my Lord,
I have never been eloquent . . . I am slow
of speech and slow of tongue.'
Exodus 4.10

Have you struggled to find the right
words over the Christmas period?

20 _____ •_____

_____

_____

20 _____ •_____

_____

_____

20 _____ •_____

_____

_____

20 _____ •_____

_____

_____

20 _____ •_____

_____

_____

_____

December

I have no greater joy than this, to hear that
my children are walking in the truth.
3 John 4

What was your most joyous moment
in the past year?

20 ___ •_____

20 ___ •_____

20 ___ •_____

20 ___ •_____

20 ___ •_____

December

29

Have you not known? Have you not heard?
The LORD is the everlasting God, the Creator
of the ends of the earth. He does not
faint or grow weary. *Isaiah 40.28*

Which aspect of God's character do
you want to praise him for today?

20 _____ •_____

_____

_____

20 _____ •_____

_____

_____

20 _____ •_____

_____

_____

20 _____ •_____

_____

_____

20 _____ •_____

_____

_____

_____

December

Neither death nor life ... nor height, nor depth, nor anything else in all creation, will be able to separate us from the love of God in Christ Jesus our Lord. *Romans 8.39*

If you could relive one moment from the past few months, what would it be?

20 _____ •_____

_____

_____

20 _____ •_____

_____

_____

20 _____ •_____

_____

_____

20 _____ •_____

_____

_____

20 _____ •_____

_____

_____

December

31

The steadfast love of the LORD never ceases,
his mercies never come to an end; they are new
every morning; great is your faithfulness.
Lamentations 3.22–23

What wonderful work has God done
in your life this year?

20 _____ •_____

_____

_____

20 _____ •_____

_____

_____

20 _____ •_____

_____

_____

20 _____ •_____

_____

_____

20 _____ •_____

_____

_____

_____